North American Kant Society Studies in Philosophy

General Editor

I0651140

Robert Loudon
University of Southern Maine

North American Kant Society Studies in Philosophy

KANT'S AESTHETICS (Vol. 1, 1991)
MINDS, IDEAS, AND OBJECTS (Vol. 2, 1992)
KANT'S EARLY METAPHYSICS (Vol. 3, 1993)
THE TABLE OF JUDGMENTS (Vol. 4, 1995/6)
LOGIC AND THE WORKINGS OF THE MIND (Vol. 5, 1997)

SELECTED ESSAYS ON KANT

By Lewis White Beck

Edited by Hoke Robinson

Introduction by Jane Kneller

**Volume 6
North American Kant Society
Studies in Philosophy**

University of Rochester Press

Rochester, New York

First published 2002
Transferred to digital printing 2009

University of Rochester Press
668 Mt. Hope Avenue, Rochester, NY 14620, USA
www.urpress.com
and Boydell & Brewer Limited
PO Box 9, Woodbridge, Suffolk IP12 3DF, UK
www.boydellandbrewer.com

ISBN-10: 1-58046-117-4
ISBN-13: 978-1-58046-117-7

Library of Congress Cataloging-in-Publication Data

Beck, Lewis White.
  [Essays. Selections. 2002]
  Selected essays on Kant/by Lewis White Beck ; edited by Hoke Robinson
    p. cm. — (North American Kant Society studies in philosophy ; v. 6)
    Includes bibliographical references and index.
    ISBN 1-58046-117-4 (alk. paper)
    1. Kant, Immanuel, 1724-1804 I. Robinson, Hoke. II. Title. III. Series.

  B2798.B344 2002
  193—dc21

                                                                    2002067305

A catalogue record for this title is available from the British Library.

This publication is printed on acid-free paper.
Printed in the United States of America

TABLE OF CONTENTS

Preface _____ vi

Introduction *by Jane Kneller* _____ vii

1. Can Kant's Synthetic Judgments Be Made Analytic? _____ 1

2. Kant's Theory of Definition _____ 17

3. Apodictic Imperatives _____ 27

4. The Fact of Reason: An Essay on Justification in Ethics _____ 45

5. Kant's Two Conceptions of the Will in their Political Context _____ 57

6. Once More unto the Breach: Kant's Answer to Hume, Again _____ 69

7. Kant and the Right of Revolution _____ 73

8. Did the Sage of Königsberg Have No Dreams? _____ 85

9. Analytic and Synthetic Judgments before Kant _____ 103

10. On the Putative Apriority of Judgments of Taste _____ 119

11. A Non Sequitur of Numbing Grossness? _____ 123

Preface

The North American Kant Society was founded at the Sixth International Kant Congress, held at the Pennsylvania State University in 1985. Lewis White Beck did not attend the congress, but his presence was felt throughout. In addition to his work selecting contributions for the congress itself, he encouraged the establishment of the Kant Society as a "sister society" to the Kant-Gesellschaft. In the years that followed he was always available with further encouragement and advice, and the Society lost a friend when he died in the summer of 1997.

Thus the suggestion that the next volume in this series be devoted to his essays was received as an opportunity both to express our gratitude for his support though the years, and to make available to younger scholars a number of essays which had strongly influenced the previous generation, and which were increasingly difficult to find. Lewis Beck represented Kant's legacy as a living and defensible philosophy back in the days when it was generally considered of merely antiquarian interest, and his work is responsible in no small measure for the Kant renaissance of the past 30 years.

We would like to thank both the publications where these essays originally appeared, and the Beck family, for permission to republish the essays. We are grateful to Jane Kneller for the introduction to the essays. And we would like to thank Rochester University Press for taking over the series from Ridgeview Publishing Company, to whom we are grateful for its publication of the previous volumes.

The following philosophy graduate students at the University of Memphis helped out by proofreading one or more of the essays: Randy Cagle, Karin Fry, Rex Gilliland, Josh Glasgow, Heath Massey, Anika Simpson, and Brad Stone. Jane Kneller caught a number of errors in reviewing the essays for her introduction.

It is with considerable pleasure that we republish here this selection of the best-known essays of Lewis White Beck.

Introduction

"...the effective refutation of an argument should not be significantly longer or any less clear than the argument itself..." ("A Non Sequitur of Numbing Grossness?")

In his reply to Lovejoy's and Strawson's criticism of Kant, Lewis White Beck succinctly describes not only his own strategy for that essay, but his life-long commitment to lucid academic style and direct, clearheaded philosophical method. Moreover, for all his scholarly insights into one of the most intricate and perplexing philosophical systems ever formulated, Beck never adopted the "piously Kantian" tone and method that sometimes mars even the best Kant scholarship. Thanks to this combination of erudition, simplicity of style and direct approach to the most difficult and important matters, Beck's work has for the past four decades facilitated students, colleagues and scholars in their efforts to comprehend Kant's daunting opus.

Lewis Beck will be certainly be long remembered for his Kant scholarship and commentary, a fact attested to by the present volume. At the same time, and through this very work, however, Beck's Kant essays reflect and advance twentieth-century philosophical concerns. Beck served as a model for generations of academic historians of philosophy by resisting the false dichotomy between philosophy and the history of philosophy prevalent among Anglo-American and Continental philosophers alike. In his work the study of the history of philosophy regularly served as a bridge to and an elucidation of contemporary philosophical debates. He had a way of making clear at every turn precisely how Kant's concerns were relevant, both in the context of the eighteenth century and in the twentieth, and students in his graduate seminars can attest to having been regularly grilled on their knowledge of current philosophical issues when interpreting the Kantian texts. From questions about the nature of analyticity to the validity of Wittgenstein's "private language argument" to the latest developments in the philosophy of science, Beck's Kant interpretation never failed to connect to the present.

At the same time, Beck remained on guard against hermeneutic anachronism. As an historian he was a dedicated empiricist, and if his historical method was in some respects "pedestrian" from the perspective of practitioners of the art, it was all the more valuable to contemporary philosophers trying to discover for themselves what aspects of the philosophical past were relevant to their own projects.

The biographical data of Beck's life have been published in several notices and memorial texts, and need only brief summary here: Educated at Emory and Duke, he moved to the University of Rochester in 1949, serving as Chair of the Philosophy Department until 1966, during which time he built a well-respected doctoral program. He was a Guggenheim Fellow, a Fellow of the American Council of Learned Societies and a Fellow and later member of the board of directors of the American Academy of Arts and Science. He published numerous influential works, including what is still the most widely read commentary on Kant's *Critique of Practical Reason*, his own *The Actor and the Spectator, Early German Philosophy*, and *Essays on Kant and Hume*.

Many of the essays in this volume are no longer in print or easily available, but are nevertheless still used widely by Kant scholars and students. The editor has done the Kant community and academics at large a real service in bringing these together in one volume. Following is a brief description of each of the essays that I hope will prove useful to those reading them for the first time.

In "Can Kant's Synthetic Judgments be Made Analytic?" Beck addresses the reasons behind Kant's insistence on a fixed, non-arbitrary distinction between analytic and synthetic judgements and the philosophical implications for Kant's work. He describes in some detail the notion of analyticity that Kant uses, pointing out that Kant himself probably made use of at least two notions (logical and psychological) of analytic judgment. Against C. I. Lewis' criticism of Kant, Beck argues that Kant was not attempting a definition of the categories of understanding since this would turn these concepts and their associated principles into claims about relations of concepts, not relations between concepts and objects. Kant was at bottom concerned to give a proof of the objective reference of certain concepts and for that a *schema*, not a definition, is necessary. Even mathematical claims, though deducible, still must rest on axioms that can be exhibited in intuition. Beck concludes that trying to revise Kant's theory to make at least mathematical judgments analytic, in keeping with much contemporary theory, would undermine Kant's view that mathematical construction is a "clue" to understanding empirical objects as determined a priori in space (geometrically).

In "Kant's Theory of Definition" Beck shows that Kant's views on the nature of analytic propositions were sufficiently different from contemporary views as to render irrelevant certain common criticisms of Kant's doctrine of synthetic judgment apriori. Definition, too, for Kant is a different notion from that employed by twentieth-century analytic philosophers. Whereas the latter tend to see definition as stipulative or nominal, Kant held that definition was the presentation of a complete concept, that is, a set of clear predicates sufficient for distinguishing the concept, where these predicates are themselves primitive and coordinate (v. subordinate). This narrower account rules out many things commonly labeled definition, and sets definition up as a goal, not a starting point, for knowledge. As Beck argues, "... real definition is a part and not merely a tool of knowledge" for Kant (p. 18). Conversely, Kant also holds that philosophers must guard against taking nominal definitions "too seriously," as if they fixed the empirical content of a concept prior to empirical investigation. This being the case, Beck argues that definition does not play the central role in Kant's account of analytic judgment that it does in later theories of analyticity. It is not necessary for certainty or justification of analytic judgments, nor do analytic judgments necessarily all follow from definitions. For this reason he concludes that Kant will not be "saved" by showing how synthetic apriori judgments can be "rendered analytic by a change in definition."

Beck addresses the odd fact that Kant distinguishes between moral rightness and categorical imperatives, but also typically speaks of categorical imperatives as moral imperatives. There is clearly a grammatical or "formal" sense in which not all imperatives are morally binding ("Shut the door." is Beck's example) and conversely, moral bindingness can be stated as a hypothetical imperative, e.g., "If you made a promise, you must keep it." In "Apodictic Imperatives" Beck carefully sorts through the general and specific classifications that Kant's theory would allow, and argues that the distinction Kant is most concerned with between imperatives is a *modal* rather than a formal or grammatical distinction, that is, it is a distinction between ways of commanding something: "an impera tive is only the mood in which a law is formulated for a being who ought to but does not by nature do what the law says a rational being would do" (p. 32). A moral imperative must command with necessity, or "apodictically," but it need not itself be commanded in categorical form. Beck shows how the modal approach allows for the possibility of apodictic hypothetical imperatives never actually discussed by Kant. What Kant calls the Categorical Imperative on this account turns out to be "a formula of an apodictic imperative *regardless of its grammatical form*" that aids us in discovering what antecedent conditions might be admissible in moral imperatives that are stated hypothetically. Allowing for the universalizability criterion to be applied to maxims that are hypothetical imperatives ("If under conditions C, do A.") opens the possibility of greater nuance and sensitivity in moral judgment than has typically been attributed to Kant's account, Beck argues.

In "Internal and External Questions" Beck argues that Kant's answer to the external question for ethics: Why be moral? lies in his account of the "fact of reason." But the nature of this doctrine is notoriously difficult to sort out. Beck argues that Kant is no intuitionist appealing to some sort of immediate and irrefutable knowledge of a truth external to the knower. That is, Kant's appeal to a "fact of reason" is not to be understood as an independent fact *for* reason, but rather as "the fact that there is pure reason": reason reflexively understands itself as practical—as giving the law to itself. Since every rational choice is at least implicitly an act of self-legislation, the external question is answered: we should be moral because we cannot but act under the idea of freedom, and that is at the same time knowledge of the moral law. We don't intuit the truth of the law, but rather enact its bindingness on us every time we make a rational choice. Thus Kant answers the external question, but as Beck points out, a Kantian answer to the external question is not (in spite of what Kant might have himself held) a justification of the internal coherence of any particular ethical system, Kantian or otherwise.

"Kant's Two Conceptions of the Will in their Political Context" is the essay in which Beck coins the useful and oft-cited phrase "Rousseauistic revolution" to describe the nature of Kant's unique and unprecedented approach to ethical theory. Kant had likened his paradigm shift in the theory of cognition to that of Copernicus' in astronomy when introducing the heliocentric view of the solar system. Rousseau's linkage of freedom and self-legislation in the political sphere was carried over by Kant into the realm of the moral, transforming ethics in the process. The essay focuses on ambiguities in Kant's notions of the will and of freedom, carefully distinguishing two kinds of will, *Wille* and *Willkür*, in Kant's philosophy. The former is a conception of the will as self-legislating, i.e., autonomous, and the latter is a conception of the will in its capacity as executor of legislation. Beck emphasizes that for Kant there are not *two* wills, but only one under different aspects, explaining the ways in which legislation and execution of laws are carried out in a single individual. Bearing in mind Kant's moral model of the will as unified under two aspects, he argues, important criticisms of Kant's political theory can be met in ways that Rousseau, whose theory of the general will was not worked out for the individual, could not.

The brevity of "Once More unto the Breach: Kant's Answer to Hume, Again" by no means correlates to the significance of this influential essay. Here Beck responds to the criticism that Kant's answer to Hume begs the question, since it is simply a regress from experience (of causal connection) that Hume doubted to the conditions necessary for the possibility of that experience. Beck denies that Kant was committing the fallacy of affirming the consequent in his reply to Hume, arguing rather that Kant was claiming that principles Hume denied (like the causal principle) are necessary conditions for the truth of claims (about the connectedness of any experience) Hume himself affirms and needs in order to make his skeptical argument in the first place. Beck concludes with a reconstruction of the argument of the Second Analogy that in its fidelity to the text and its inherent plausibility remains one of the best to date.

In "Kant and the Right of Revolution" Beck explains Kant's apparently contradictory views on the right to rebellion against and overthrow of established governments. By examining Kant's opposition to revolution on legal grounds, his theoretical political commitments and their influence on his interpretation of the 1789 revolution, and his extrasystematic grounds for sympathizing with the revolution, Beck tries to dissolve at least some of the tensions in Kant's political views. That beginnings (legal or not) don't matter, that the sovereignty of the monarch disappears permanently when s/he (always illegitimately) relinquishes it to the people, that Kant's censure was directed not at the Estates General and revolution, but against restoration of the monarchy and interventions from outside to aid in that restoration, are all elements that help us understand the exigencies of Kant's politics. In the end, Beck argues, Kant's views can only be made plausible by recourse to his moral teleology, and even then all inconsistency is not removed, since the latter remains in tension with the demands of individual morality.

In "Did the Sage of Königsberg have no Dreams?" Beck shows how Kant could consistently and plausibly answer this question posed by C.I. Lewis. Although it is clear (thanks to Kemp Smith) that Kant did consider dreams part of conscious experience (along with non-categorized human mental states as well as animals' mental states), the argument for this needs to be given, and is not obvious, given the claim of the B-edition deduction that all consciousness is subject to the categories. What Beck points out is that "subject to the categories" need not mean that in every instance a given experience must be categorized, but that experience, if it is to be anything at all for me, must contain *some* representations that are categorized, that is, related to an object, and that *all* representations, objective or not, must be capable of being held in one consciousness. The difficult doctrine of "judgments of perception" is dealt with by placing it in the context of Kant's working out the answer to Lewis-type questions between the first and second editions of the first *Critique* and by relating judgments of perception to judgments of sense in Kant's "Critique of Aesthetic Judgment". Here Kant addresses the problem of the first *Critique* (paragraph 13) directly: the conditions of subsumability of specific concepts under general ones, and the fit between what is given to sensibility and our cognitive apparatus are, for Kant, contingent facts. Nature might have been so constituted that it never gave our cognitive faculties occasion to come into play. Thus Beck argues, subjective experiences of many sorts, including dreams, are explicable for Kant.

In "Analytic and Synthetic Judgments before Kant" Beck looks at the accusation made by Lovejoy, but also much earlier by a contemporary of Kant's, Eberhard, that synthetic judgments a priori were distinguished already in Wolff, and that Kant was therefore not presenting anything novel (except for the terminology itself) in his introduction of these judgments into his philosophy. Beck carefully sorts through what Kant did and did not attribute to his predecessors vis-à-vis the analytic/synthetic distinction. He points out that something akin to this distinction was already at work not only in Wolff, but in Leibniz and even in Hume. Hume's account of relations of ideas in the *Treatise* is not one based strictly on the test of logical nonsense (i.e., its denial involves a logical contradiction) but also on "unimaginability and even counterintuitivity," Beck argues. In other words, something like what Kant would have called synthetic judgments a priori were implicit in Hume's account of relations of ideas. Beck further argues that in his more sophisticated work Leibniz also failed to maintain a strict division between analytic a priori on the one hand and synthetic a posteriori on the other. Beck concludes by arguing that if anyone had predated Kant in making explicit the analytic/synthetic distinction, and also arguing that synthetic judgments were possible a priori, it was Wolff's critic, Crusius.

"On the Putative Apriority of Judgments of Taste" is another brief but useful essay in which Beck tackles a large problem for Kant's justification of aesthetic reflective judgment. He begins with the simple observation that empirical judgments cannot be made a priori, but they can have necessary universal validity, if true. This is because for Kant, they may presuppose a judgment a priori. Judgments of experience are like judgments of taste in this respect: both are empirical and hence a posteriori, but both, if true, depend upon judgments a priori. In the case of the former these "judgments" are the categories, in the case of the latter the principle of reflective judgment. Keeping in mind that objectivity, or universal necessary validity, and truth are not the same, it is clear that an empirical claim about aesthetic experience can be false. Just as in cognitive empirical claims the cognizer might employ the categories incorrectly, so in aesthetic empirical claims the aesthetic appreciator might incorrectly invoke the conditions of aesthetic judgment, falsely assuming that s/he was guided by disinterest when in fact a covert interest was involved.

Finally in "A Non Sequitur of Numbing Grossness?" Beck responds to the accusation made by Lovejoy and again by Strawson that Kant proceeds to infer the objective succession of representations from their subjective succession (how things are from how they appear to us), a clear *non sequitur*. Beck carefully explains what looks like an egregious failure of philosophical acumen by appeal to his own earlier interpretation of the Second Analogy as an answer to Hume (and the fact that Kant also explicitly denies that a move from subjective to objective series can be made). Beck points out that whether or not Kant manages here to establish the truth of the causal principle, what is at issue in the charge of *non sequitur* is whether Kant begs the question against Hume. He shows that Kant's argument involves the claim that Hume's own premises make use of appeal to past cases of sequences of representations, and that this very appeal requires a means (a law) for recognition of those as genuine *sequences* (not co-existents). No Humean question is begged and the charge of gross *non sequitur* does not hold.

■■■

As a former doctoral student and later collaborator and colleague of Lewis White Beck, it is impossible to end this introduction without a personal commemorative note of gratitude and expression of great affection for the philosopher and educator whose work continues to inspire and guide my own. Lewis was a wonderful mentor and, once the hurdles were jumped and the official titles achieved, a real friend. I know I speak for his many former students when I say he will be sorely missed and remembered fondly.

Fort Collins
June, 2000

Can Kant's Synthetic Judgments Be Made Analytic?

In the 1760's, when Kant had first drawn his distinction between analytic and synthetic judgments, he made the following note: "If one had the entire concept of which the notions of the subject and predicate are *compars*, synthetic judgments would change into analytic. It is a question of how much arbitrariness there is."[1] This question has been asked repeatedly since that time, and the clear and unmistakable trend of the answers has been that the decision whether a specific judgment is analytic or synthetic is arbitrary or at least is dependent upon variable conditions of how much the judger knows about the subject of the judgment and on his arbitrary decision of the choice and formula of his definitions.

In recent discussions of the distinction, analytic judgments are those that follow from explicit definitions by the rules of logic; and definitions are nominal or stipulative, to some degree arbitrary. If it is further argued, as is often done, that all a priori judgments are analytic, it follows that the distinction between a priori and a posteriori is likewise a shifting, arbitrary distinction.

Kant, who first asked the question, seems to have decided very early that the line of demarcation between these two types of judgment was *not* variable or arbitrary. The purpose of this essay is to inquire into the reasons for his decision and to indicate some of its implications for his philosophy as a whole.

ANALYTIC AND SYNTHETIC JUDGMENTS

Judgment, for Kant, is a synthesis of representations, having objective validity. The synthesis must be in accord with some objective, normative rule, and not merely illustrate some contingent law of association. A representation, functioning in the synthesis of judgment, is not just a brute given mental content, but is a mark of an object, its meaning fixed by a rule. Abstraction from the given complexity of representations in consciousness, and the generalization that a particular kind of representation is the mark of a particular kind of object, are necessary in converting raw representations into marks which can be manipulated in knowing.[2] Concepts are such marks functioning in knowledge; they are representations under an analytical (abstractive) unity through which they are discursive and not merely given sense contents. As concepts, they are not given; they are made concepts by being involved in a special attitude of intention and the interpretation of data. All that we directly have of an object is such marks. Our original consciousness is a congeries of raw materials for concepts, and the business of consciousness is to refine and organize these representations, assigning to some of them the role of subjects and to others that of predicates in judgments which are their objectively valid syntheses;[3] only as predicates of possible judgments do *Vorstellungen* serve as concepts, and only as containing representations under themselves do concepts refer to objects.[4]

Besides the analytical unity by which *hic et nunc* representations are made to serve as marks under a discursive concept (e.g., this *quale* at this time is seen as an example of a specific quality also instanced in another *quale* at another time), in order that there be judgment there must also be a synthetical unity through which the concepts (and their corresponding representations) are referred to the same object.

This object may not be given at all, or if given it is given as only a still further complex of representations which refer to "the same object" only by virtue of some precedent synthetical unity. The synthetical unity, which is a form and not a content of experience, is not given, but is prescribed to experience by a rule that requires a common focus of meaning of the several concepts that appear in a judgment; if one such object is not meant by the various concepts, the synthesis of the concepts is a comparison, a setting of them side by side, and not a judgment. This common object is called by Kant X, and the rule of synthetical unity means that the terms in a judgment (concepts, derived through the analytical unity of representations), such as A and B, must be regarded as marks of X. Then through A and B we know X, and the cognition of X through A or B is a concept of X.[5] A and B are, epistemologically, predicates of X, but one of them is made to serve as the logical subject and the other as the logical predicate. The one called subject is directly related to X, the one called predicate is indirectly related to X in the judgment, though its occurrence in experience may be direct evidence of the existence of X (usually it is the wider concept, and is applied to a specific X only through the mediation of the subject concept).[6] Thus, to summarize and make specific: when X is known through two concepts related to each other in a synthetical unity, then a judgment whose form is given by a category or rule of this synthetical unity is established. If the rule is, for instance, the category of inherence and subsistence, the judgment reads, "There is an X such that X is A and X is B."

If B is related to A directly by being included as a part of its connotation, so that "X is A" implies logically "X is B," the judgment is analytic. In an analytic judgment, reference to X is otiose, and we say simply, "All A is B" where A and B are "partial concepts" of X, and B is a constitutive part of A. But "All A is B" is an elliptical expression since A is a complex concept containing B. Fully expanded, therefore, the analytic judgment is the tautology, "All $A.B$ is B."

When B is a concept of X because it is a *nota notae* of X, i.e., a mark or constituent of A, we can speak of the judgment as one in which the certainty of the connection of subject and predicate is "through identity."[7] If the identity is explicit, the judgment is inconsequential. The important case is the one in which the identity is implicit, so that its explication "widens our knowledge *formaliter*" though not *materialiter*. B may be "covertly contained in the concept"[8] and not thought "so distinctly and with the same (full) consciousness" as A.[9] It is an "analytic attribute" of A contained in it and elicited from it by logical analysis.[10] But it is essential that it be "contained in" A, so that the judgment is explicative, not ampliative, and independent of further experience of the X of which both A and B are concepts.

Now if the decision on analyticity of a specific judgment could be based on a definition of the subject, it would be easy enough to determine whether the judgment is analytic. But Kant rejects this procedure, because he holds that "definability" is a stricter condition than "analyzability," and that we can therefore make analytical judgments with concepts we cannot define. It is, in fact, through organizing analytic judgments that we gradually approach to definition,[11] which is the end, not the beginning, of knowledge.

Since Kant has so restricted the scope and value of definition, these statements about the inclusion of one concept in another are exceedingly obscure. It seems that, without a stated definition, they can be understood in part only psychologically or phenomenologically. Speaking for the phenomenological interpretation is the emphasis upon what is "actually thought" in the subject; speaking for a logical interpretation is the fact that analytic attributes may be uncovered and brought to light only by sustained inquiry, and are not present, in any phenomenological sense, in the thought of the concept of the subject.

If we investigate each phrase in these passages, the possible confusion of the two meanings is not removed. For instance, "contained in" (*enthalten in*) was a logical term used by Kant's contemporaries to describe predicates belonging to all individuals denoted by a concept.[12] But Kant obviously does not mean it only in a logical sense, for then synthetic attributes would be contained in the subject concept, which he denies; "contained in" seems to have reference to the subjective intension, and thus to have at least psychological overtones. But the words "actually thought in the concept of the subject" are elsewhere given a strictly logical meaning, since Kant says that what is really thought in a concept is "nothing other than its definition."[13]

I think we have to suspect here a fundamental failure on Kant's part to distinguish the logical from the phenomenological aspects of thought. Where definitions or fairly complete analyses are available, he thinks of the distinction between analytic and synthetic judgment as logical; where they are not, but are rather the objects of search, he has recourse to a phenomenological criterion, by virtue of which he seeks definitions through analysis of what, in the plainest sense, is "actually thought" in a concept or even "contained in" a complex experience subject to subsequent analysis.[14]

While we cannot speak of two definitions of the analytic, and can at most say that the analytic has both a logical and a phenomenological dimension, we can discern two criteria for analytic judgment. Kant, in apparent disregard of their differences, uses first one and then the other as it suits his purposes, perhaps in the conviction that their answers will in any specific case be the same.

1) The logical criterion of analytic judgment is its conformity to the law of contradiction, a necessary condition of any judgment and a necessary and sufficient condition for an analytic judgment. The test is applied as follows: substitute in a judgment synonyms for synonyms, or an analysis or definition of the

subject concept for the subject itself. Then the contradictory of this judgment will infringe the law of contradiction if the original judgment is analytic. And as the contradictory of a self-contradictory proposition is necessary, the original judgment is necessary.

In applying the logical criterion, a definition in the strict sense is not required, for it is from the analytic judgments in informal exposition that we first gain the definition. All that is needed is a partial analysis of the subject concept. The absence of definition may at most prevent only the decision that some specific judgment is *not* analytic,[15] for what is mentioned as the predicate may be an unnoticed analytic attribute that we would have noticed had we possessed a full definition. But no criterion is infallible; even given a strict definition, the pertinancy of a specific attribute as analytical may be a discovery of the most difficult and surprising kind. It is in such cases that there will be the greatest divergence between decisions made on this and those made on the phenomenological criterion.

2) The phenomenological criterion is the issue of an inspection of what is found introspectively to be really thought in the concept of the subject. Though we have seen that what is "really thought" is said to be a definition, and that the mention of predicates not thought "with the same (full) consciousness" suggests a very wide range of predicates that might pass the logical but fail the phenomenological test, still it is clear that Kant was not free from a psychologizing, introspective tendency in his decisions on what is analytic and what is synthetic. The *Port-Royal Logic*[16] demanded "moderate attention" to see whether the predicate is "truly contained in the idea of the subject," and not a completely articulated logical system as a criterion for this decision; the same kind of "moderate attention" seems to provide a criterion for Kant. He repeatedly asks himself and the reader what he thinks when he thinks a particular concept, and though undoubtedly one may think much, by casual association, which is not "contained in the concept," what he does *not* think is *not* included in the content of the concept.

Just as he has previously distinguished between what is contained in and what is contained under a concept, so also he distinguishes what "lies in" a concept and what "belongs to" it.[17] There seems to be here a tacit distinction between two kinds of concepts, one being a concept of a highly refined analytical or abstractive unity, subject to strict definition, and the other being a looser complex of representations, more or less loosely held together and expandable through the accretion of new experience or subject to restriction in content through the supervention of a definition.[18]

I now turn, for the space of one paragraph, to Kant's description of synthetic judgments, after which I shall come back to these two criteria of analytic judgment. The following material is essential for evaluating the issues raised by the two criteria.

B may be related to *A* indirectly by virtue of the fact that both are predicates of the same *X*. Then the concept *A* does not include the concept of *B* as a part of its logical essence, and to relate them to each other in judgment requires reference to the X of which each is a partial concept. There are three kinds of X which serve to mediate between A and B. (1) X may be a schema of an object in general (of a thing, cause, etc.). (2) X may be a determinable intuition of space or time or both, which A and B both refer to and make determinate. (3) X may be a datum or *concretum* of experience, "the complete experience of the object which I think through the concept A."[19] In the former two cases, the judgment will be valid regardless of the empirical content of the concepts, and in the first case there is established the kind of judgment which appears in "metaphysics as science." Failure to provide a schema without the conditions of space and time and to put the thing in itself in the role of the X makes synthetic judgments impossible except of objects of possible experience. The second is the situation with respect to mathematical judgments, where X is a construction. In the third alternative, the judgment is a posteriori. But in each case it is a synthetic judgment, since the predicate is not found by analysis of the logical subject. If X is (as is actually the case) a subjective condition for the synthesis of A and B, the resulting synthetic judgment is, in the transcendental sense, only subjectively valid; though we can say still that the predicate is a part of the real and not of the nominal essence. In the same sense, an analytic judgment is objectively and even transcendently valid, not being restricted to the conditions of synthesis placed upon the X.[20]

From this account of the origin of synthetic judgment and from the two criteria mentioned above, it is clear that the distinction between analytic and synthetic judgment is not one of formal logic, for formal logic abstracts from the meaning of all terms.

VARIABILITY OF THE DISTINCTION

Eberhard interpreted an analytic judgment as one the predicate of which is an *essentia* of the subject, and a synthetic judgment as one whose predicate is an attribute derived from an *essentia*. But Kant denies that this is his meaning, for he holds that "derived from" is equivocal. If the attribute is derived by logical analysis, the judgment is indeed analytic whether we *knew* that the attribute was "contained in" the subject concept or not; but there are other attributes, synthetic attributes (*Bestimmungen*), that are not contained in the logical essence, even though they might be associated with it in our minds, e.g., as weight with body. They are derived not by logical analysis but by construction or exhibition of a corresponding intuitive object. From such an experience the attribute can as it were be read off, though it is not a *nota notae* of the subject concept but a nota of the real object. It is this kind of synthetic predicate which is a part of the *ratio essendi* of the object, and it gives the concept of the subject and all its judgments whatever objective validity they have.

Though Eberhard was a mediocre thinker, much of whose argument is vitiated by being based upon patent misunderstandings of Kant, he did nevertheless ask a difficult and important question, "How do we decide what is 'actually thought' in a concept?" Unless a definite and plausible criterion can be given that is exempt from the vagaries of the phenomenological criterion and of the logical criterion when Kant attempts to employ it unarmed with definitions, then an important member of the structure of his philosophy must be given up. Modern writers, reacting against both psychologism and phenomenology, wanting a behavioral rather than an introspectional criterion if a significant logical criterion cannot be given, have directed their main attack on the possibility of maintaining the distinction, in any particular instance, without a complement of definitions.

Rather than considering the views of those who give up or relativize the distinction for the reasons just mentioned, however, it will be more profitable to consider the views of a critic who admits a sharp distinction between analytic and synthetic, yet who does not base it on the test of nominal or stipulative definition. A critic this close to Kant is likely to be more instructive, at this juncture, than one more radically opposed to Kant. The criticism I shall consider is that by C. I. Lewis, which is in part an infinitely improved version of some debating points raised by Eberhard. Kant's cognizance of these arguments, admittedly in a more primitive form, makes a study of them especially worthwhile for an understanding of Kant himself.

Lewis argues as follows. The notion of a necessary but nonanalytic proposition such as "Every event has a cause" is based on an equivocation. For "event," as a concept which does not contain "having a cause" as a part of its meaning, is not the same as the concept of "event" which does contain the concept "having a cause." Part of Kant's argument is based on the former and simpler concept, and here Kant rightly infers that the proposition is synthetic. But the argument that the proposition is a priori is based on the second, richer, concept. We can, according to Kant, think without contradiction an uncaused event; hence the relation expressed in the judgment is synthetic; but we cannot imagine, represent, or know an event as objective without relating it to another event by a rule of causation; hence the judgment is known a priori.

The equivocation is that "event" in the second case means "phenomenal event in objective space and time," while in the first case it is not so restricted. If this restriction is made explicit, however, the relation between the restricted concepts is seen to be analytic. The second Analogy of Experience seems to be synthetic only because the word "event" is not usually given the restricted meaning. The term needs to be fixed by definition before one can pronounce the judgment to be analytic or synthetic; and in defining it, we must be sure to include in its meaning everything needed to determine the objective applicability of the term in question: "...Anything which is essential to the temporal character of an event must be included in the adequate concept of it as a temporal event.... A definition which does not logically entail all characters essential to what is defined, is faulty."[21]

Kant's reply to this kind of criticism, as it appeared in its first crude form, or rather Schultz's reply written under Kant's supervision, makes two responses.

1) Two different propositions, one of which is analytic and one synthetic, may be expressed by the same sentence, for the same word in the sentences may refer to two different concepts, one narrower and one broader.

2) Closely related to this is the assertion of the "fixity" of a concept. A concept cannot be arbitrarily widened through the accumulation of information. It can be replaced by another called by the same name; but of any given concept it can be decided what is implicit in it to be explicated in analytical judgment and what does not lie in it at all. When one changes a definition, which may change the status of many judgments, the judgments are changed not merely in status but in meaning and validity. Definitions should not, therefore, be arbitrarily changed; a new one must pass the same kind of test of "realness" that the old one originally passed and later failed, if it is not to be merely stipulation without objective reference. We cannot convert empirical knowledge into a priori knowledge simply by refining our language:

> Let one put into the concept of the subject just so many attributes that the predicate which one wishes to prove of the subject can be derived from its concept merely by the law of contradiction. The critical philosophy permits him to make this kind of analytic judgment, but raises a question about the concept of the subject itself. It asks: how did you come to include in this concept the different attributes so that it [now analytically] entails synthetic propositions? First prove the objective reality of your concept, i.e., first prove that any one of its attributes really belongs to a possible object, and when you have done that, then prove that the other attributes belong to the same thing that the first one belongs to, without themselves belonging to the first attribute. The whole question of how much or how little the concept of the subject is to contain has not the least bearing on the metaphysical question: How are synthetic a priori judgments possible? It belongs merely in the logical theory of definition. And the theory of definition without doubt requires that one not introduce more attributes into a definition than are necessary to distinguish the defined thing from all others. Hence [in a good definition] one excludes those attributes of which one can demand a proof whether and on what grounds they belong to the former attributes [that *are* included].[22]

Put in our own words, Kant is saying that a definition which will change a synthetic into an analytic judgment must be either nominal or real. If nominal, it does not in the least affect the cognitive status of the original judgment; while it may make the original sentence formally analytic, it does not give to the knowledge it expresses any logical or epistemic necessity it previously lacked.[23] And if the definition is a real one, we must know the necessary conjunction of independent, coordinate attributes in order to make it; and this conjunction is precisely what was stated in the synthetic judgment whose status is now being disputed. All that is effected by such a procedure, we might say, is that the locus of a priori synthesis is shifted.

INDEFINABILITY OF THE CATEGORIES

Thus far I have considered only Kant's explicit answers to the criticism that the analytic-synthetic distinction is variable. I now examine Kant's reply in its general philosophical bearings.

I have already mentioned that there are in Kant's writings two quite different species of concept. In one case, like that of "water," the word is "more properly to be regarded as merely a designation than as a concept of the thing,"[24] and its meaning does vary with experience. In the other, the concept is fixed either by definition, or fixed because it is a *pure* concept which, while not subject to definition, is not subject to revision by the accumulation of experience. In the latter case, Kant believed that a fixed decision could be made concerning what was and what was not included in it, even at a time before a stated definition had been reached. The rationalistic tradition in which Kant wrote fixed many of the most important concepts by "implicit" definition and common use or by nominal definitions that had become well established.[25] Thus Kant could confidently decide that a given proposition is analytic without the necessity of referring to a "rule book" of stipulative definitions. We, in a more conventionalistic period, are usually puzzled by some of his decisions, and can only feel that Kant and his contemporaries were committing what Whitehead called the "fallacy of the perfect dictionary"—when the dictionary could not, in principle, exist for Kant at all. But the more important point is that the concepts with which Kant is most concerned, viz., the categories, are not fixed by definition and need not be fixed in this way. They are fixed because, as pure, they are not susceptible to experiential modification.

Let us consider what Kant was attempting to do with these concepts. It had been shown by Hume that they could not be given objective validity by definition, and though Kant might have given a richer, more determinate definition to such a concept as cause, a still more extended Humean argument would have been fatal again to its claims to objective validity. Definition and proof of objective validity are not the same except in mathematics; which, for quite peculiar reasons, does not have to meet the Humean type of criticism. Assuming a broader definition, a proof of the objective validity of its analytic consequences is still called for if Hume's criticisms of the rational structure of empirical knowledge are to be met. Given the broader definition, of course, antecedently synthetic judgments become analytic. So long as the definitional component is expanded ad lib, any a priori judgment can be shown to be analytic. But apriority is not dependent upon this kind of analyticity; the analyticity of such a judgment is not a condition of its apriority but a subsequent, factitious addendum to it. That is, there must be recognition of some special dignity of function of a specific proposition that makes it worthwhile to devise a language in which it will be necessary; but the linguistic necessity is established subsequent to this recognition.

Kant did not simply suppose that causality had objective meaning; he tried to show that it did, and in doing so he found that he had to add to the concept of sufficient reason determinations which neither Hume nor the rationalists had suspected; he had to give a new interpretation to "possible experience" as the mediator between the terms of such a judgment. To have suppressed this interpretation for the sake of a formal definition of cause which would render the second Analogy of Experience analytical would have distorted the whole procedure of the critical philosophy, and would have left unanswered the reiterated question, how can *this* judgment, based on definition, be valid objectively?

Kant thought that real definitions should come at the end of inquiry, not at the beginning. One might expect, therefore, that the contribution of the *Critique of Pure Reason* might have been seen as a new set of definitions subsequent to which a priori judgments previously called synthetic would now be called analytic. Why did Kant not see his work in this way, but obstinately regarded the Analogies as synthetic judgments—in spite of the fact that he might have seen the logical classification as tentative, dependent upon the richness of the concepts?

There were several reasons why Kant did not do this. Among them was his respect for tradition; more important was his recognition that Hume's objections to the rational foundations of empirical knowledge could not be met by new definitions. And a still more fundamental reason is to be found in his repeated denials of the definability of the categories: the definitions which some might think would serve for this reduction of all a priori knowledge to analytic knowledge cannot be given. Definitions, however elaborated, are still conceptual relations; but what is needed is some way to get a concept into relation with an object, and to do it in an a priori fashion. Concepts alone, however richly furnished with predicates, do not establish contact with things; only intuition can provide this contact. We can indeed conceptualize and name the requisite intuition; but in doing this, we treat it like a universal concept, and as such it fails to establish the objective reference. It always leaves open the question: does *this* complex universal apply? The category, whether it can be defined or not, must be schematized—must be provided, in Lewis' terminology, with a sense meaning as well as a linguistic meaning. Kant is profuse in his definitions of pure categories, but these definitions are nominal.[26] Schematizing a category is very different front defining it:

> There is something strange and even nonsensical in the notion that there should be a concept which must have a meaning but which cannot be defined. But the categories are in a unique position, for only by virtue of the *general condition of sensibility* can they have a definite meaning and relation to an object. This condition, however,

is omitted in the pure category, for this can contain only the logical function of bringing the manifold under a concept,[27]

without specifying the concept or the condition of its application to a specific manifold.

No philosopher has emphasized more than Kant the fundamental difference between sense and understanding while at the same time asserting their complementary function. This fundamental difference is essential here. It is not the *concept* of an intuitive condition, which might be added to a concept or included in its definition, that gives full meaning to the category; it is the *condition of sensibility* itself,[28] the condition of its actual use in specific circumstances according to rule. This is a transcendental addendum, a real predicate, a synthetic predicate, a *Bestimmung*, an element in the *ratio essendi* as well as the *ratio cognoscendi*. It is not just another attribute without which the definition is "inadequate." Make the added condition a conceptual amendment to the definition, and the entire question is postponed: we would still have to ask, "How does *this* concept have a priori objective application?"[29]

Because Kant does admit definitions, in the strictest sense, only in the field of mathematics,[30] it is easy to admit a sharp distinction between analytic and synthetic judgments here; in fact, mathematical definition has been taken as establishing the paradigm of the analytic-synthetic distinction.[31] Granting the sharpness of the distinction between analytic and synthetic here, most competent critics of Kant are in agreement that he was in error in saying that mathematical judgments are synthetic. It is said that what kept him from seeing that they are analytic was the lack of adequate mathematical definitions, definitions not available until much later. Professor Lewis characteristically writes: "It would be ungrateful and unjust to blame Kant for not foreseeing that, from genuinely adequate mathematical definitions, the theorems of mathematics might be deducible."[32] Obviously, deducible from definition and analytic are here regarded as equivalent notions.

This however, as we have amply seen, is not what Kant meant by "analytic." In the *Prolegomena* he wrote:

> ...as it was found that the conclusions of mathematicians all proceed according to the law of contradiction...men persuaded themselves that the fundamental principles were known from the same law. This was a great mistake, for a synthetical proposition can indeed be established [*eingesehen*] by the law of contradiction, but only by presupposing another synthetical proposition from which it follows, never by that law alone.[33]

From this we see the following: (1) Mathematical theorems may be synthetic even if proved by the law of contradiction, i.e., by strictly logical procedure. Deducibility is not a sufficient condition for analyticity. To be analytic, in Kant's meaning, a proposition would have to be proven by the law of contradiction *alone*, i.e., its contradictory would have to be *self*-contradictory; but in mathematical proof by strict logic, the contradictory of the proposition contradicts some *other* assumed propositions. (2) A proposition will be called synthetic if among its premises is a synthetic proposition, such as an axiom, or a mathematical definition, i.e., a synthetical definition which can be exhibited in a construction. (3) Mathematical axioms (fundamental principles) are synthetic since they are not established by the analysis of a given concept, but only by the intuitive construction of the concept, which will show the necessary presence of attributes not included in a logical definition of the subject.[34]

The theorems, therefore, can be called synthetic even though they are strictly (analytically, in modern usage) demonstrable. The famous discussion of the example, "7 + 5 = 12," two paragraphs later, is quite independent of the grounds given in the quotation for calling the theorems synthetic. It is, in fact, inconsistent with it. In the quotation, Kant is conceding that a theorem does follow from premises by strict logic; whatever may be the nature of the premises, the internal structure of the proof is logical. But in the discussion of "7 + 5" Kant is arguing that a theorem does not follow logically even from synthetic axioms, but that intuitive construction enters into the theorem itself and its proof. These two theses—that an intuitive synthetic element is present in the primitive propositions, and that an intuitive synthetic process is present in demonstration—are independent of each other. Because a mathematical judgment is often synthetical by the phenomenological criterion, Kant seems to have supposed that there were good logical reasons for calling it synthetic. Of these two theses, only the first is of any moment in the epistemology (not the methodology) of mathematical knowledge, but it is only the second of the theses that could be corrected by the use of what Lewis calls "genuinely adequate mathematical definitions."

The real dispute between Kant and his critics is not whether the theorems are analytic in the sense of being strictly deducible, and not whether they should be called analytic now when it is admitted that they are deducible from definitions, but whether there are any primitive propositions which are synthetic and intuitive. Kant is arguing that the axioms cannot be analytic, both because they must establish a connection between concepts, just as definitions do, and because they must establish a connection that can be exhibited in intuition. And this is what is denied by the modern critic of Kant.

I think Kant is obviously right in saying that there cannot be a system of nothing but analytic propositions; there must be some complexes to analyze, and these must be stated synthetically. But if the postulates are not analytic, this does not mean that they are synthetic *propositions*, i.e., synthetic statements expressing truths. A stipulation can "establish" synthetic relations, but it does not thereby qualify as a proposition. If it be assumed that mathematics is a game, then the analytic-synthetic distinction is of no importance in discussing the postulates, because the premises are not propositions at all but are only stipulations or propositional functions.[35]

Kant did not espouse the game theory. Mathematics was for him objective knowledge. That is why he regarded the axioms as propositions, not proposals. Were they mere relations of ideas, in Hume's sense, they could be made as "adequate" as one wished, yet the question of how they could be objectively valid would remain untouched. But for Kant, real mathematical definitions are possible, because the definition creates the object. This sounds like stipulation again; but the object is not an arbitrary logical product of subjectively chosen independent properties. To define a mathematical concept is to prescribe rules for its construction in space and time. Such a definition is a synthetical proposition, because the spatial determination of the figure is not a logical consequence of the concept but is a real condition of its application. The real property is joined to the logical properties synthetically, not analytically.

Objections to Kant's views of mathematics, therefore, cannot be removed merely by the substitution of more adequate sets of definitions and postulates, as if being a better mathematician would have corrected Kant's philosophy of mathematics. *The syntheticity of mathematical knowledge in Kant is not a consequence of the inadequacy of his definitions.* It is an essential feature of his entire theory of mathematical knowledge, by which the identity of mathematics and logic was denied. Mathematical knowledge in his view of the world has objective reference, and this is obtained not through definition but through intuition and construction. His mathematical definitions are real; what is deduced from them may be, in modern but not Kantian terminology, analytic propositions. But the propositions admitted as theorems by Kant are not like the analytic propositions of modern mathematics or the relations of ideas of Hume, for they have a necessary relation to experience through the synthetic, intuitive character of the definitions and axioms. Even propositions which Kant admits are analytic belong to mathematics only if they can be exhibited in intuition.[36] Whatever improvements in Kant's definitions might have been introduced for the sake of making the theorems analytic in his sense would have cost a high price in setting mathematics apart from the discussion of the conditions of possible experience. And had they been seen as analytic, Kant's long and deep concern with mathematics would not have positively contributed to his interpretation of the problems of empirical knowledge. For Kant saw in mathematics a clue to the objectivity of all a priori knowledge, both analytic and what he considered to be synthetic. This is indeed the sense of the Copernican Revolution: even empirical objects are constructions; and their necessary conditions are geometrical. Had Kant radically sundered mathematical knowledge from the intuitive a priori structures of empirical knowledge, as he criticizes Hume for doing,[37] both would have been rendered unintelligible to him. The question is thereby raised whether, in introducing modern amendments into Kant's theory of mathematics (perhaps for the purpose of "saving what is essential in the critical philosophy"), we do not at the same time overlook or destroy everything distinctive in his theory of empirical knowledge.[38]

NOTES

1. *Reflection* 3928 (Academy edn., XVII, 350).
2. *Reflection* 2881.
3. See *Reflections* 3920, 4634.
4. *Critique of Pure Reason* A 69=B 94.
5. *Reflection* 3920.
6. *The Progress of Metaphysics*, Academy edn., XX, 274.
7. *Lectures on Logic*, §36 (Academy edn., IX, 111). Kant objects to calling them identical judgments, however; see *Über eine Entdeckung*, Academy edn., VIII, 244.
8. *Critique of Pure Reason*, A 7=B 10
9. *Prolegomena*, §2 a.
10. *Über eine Entdeckung*, Academy edn., VIII, 228-29.
11. *Prolegomena*, §2 c 3; see also *Lectures on Logic*, §109, Note; *Prize Essay,* Academy edn., II, 282; *False Subtlety of the Four Syllogistic Figures*, Academy edn., II, 61. I have studied the relation between Kant's theory of definition and the distinction between the analytic and synthetic in some detail in "Kant's Theory of Definition" [pp. 17-26 below].
12. Hans Vaihinger, *Commentar zu Kants Kritik der reinen Vernunft* (2 vols.; Stuttgart: W. Spemann, 1881), I, 258. "Contained in" is contrasted with "contained under" (*Reflection* 3043). The latter, used in describing synthetic judgments, seems to mean for Kant what Vaihinger says was commonly meant by "contained in." See also *Reflections* 2896, 2902.
13. *Critique of Pure Reason*, A 718=B 746.
14. A recent paper by Robert S. Hartman, "Analytic and Synthetic as Categories of Inquiry," in *Perspectives in Philosophy* (Ohio State University, 1953), pp. 55-57, has the special merit of singling out the two kinds of analyticity, one of which it calls definitional and the other expositional, and distinguishing both from "analytic" in the sense of descriptive of what is "contained in" an experience of an empirical object. Hartman's paper presents very clearly the processes by which analytic judgments lead to definitions, and definitions then establish a new and stricter criterion of analyticity. Another study of the process by which an analytic judgment may become synthetic is K. Sternberg, "Über die Unterscheidung von analytischen und synthetischen Urteilen," *Kant-Studien*, XXXI (1926), 171-201.
15. See *Lectures on Logic*, §109, Note.
16. Part IV, ch. 6.
17. *Critique of Pure Reason*, A 718=B 746; but cf. *Lectures on Logic*, Introduction, VIII (Academy edn, IX, 61) where attributes belong to the essence, so far as they are derived from it.
18. The confusion between these two meanings of "concept" has been discussed by W. Koppelmann, "Kants Lehre vom analytischen Urteil," *Philosophische Monatshefte*, XXI (1885), 65-101; and by H. Ritzel, "Über analytische Urteile," *Jahrbuch f. Philosophie u. phänomenologische Forschung*, III (1916), see especially pp. 261-76, 324. The full significance of it, as representing the interpenetration of two stages of inquiry domi-

nated respectively by the analytic and the synthetic method, is ably worked out by Hartman, "Analytic and Synthetic as Categories of Inquiry."

19. *Critique of Pure Reason*, A 8; omitted in B.

20. *Reflection* 3950.

21. C. I. Lewis, *An Analysis of Knowledge and Valuation* (La Salle: Open Court Publishing Co., 1947), pp. 161-62. 1 have given a fuller exposition of Lewis' views (without discussion of the point raised here) in "Die Kantkritik von C. I. Lewis und der analytischen Schule," *Kant-Studien*, XLV (1954), 3-20.

22. *Rezension von Eberhards Magazin*, Academy edn., XX, 408-9.

23. In this, Lewis is in agreement with Kant. In criticizing those who identify the a priori and the analytic, and then define the analytic in terms of linguistic rules or procedures, Lewis writes: "If implications of conceptions of this sort should be well worked out, it must appear that they are fatal to the thesis that what is a priori coincides with what is analytic; since the notion that what may be known true without recourse to sense experience, is relative to vocabulary or dependent on conventions of procedure, is not credible" (*Analysis of Knowledge and Valuation*, p. 36).

24. *Critique of Pure Reason*, A 728=B 756.

25. See J. H. Hyslop, "Kant's Treatment of Analytic and Synthetic Judgment," *The Monist*, XIII (1903), 331-51, which emphasizes Cartesian and Newtonian conclusions as they "infected" the concepts Kant used.

26. *Critique of Pure Reason*, A 244=B 302.

27. *Ibid.*, A 244-45; omitted from B. Italics supplied.

28. The difference between a concept of an intuitive condition and the intuitive condition itself is formally like that between the concept of existence and existence itself. Kant's criticism of the ontological argument, *mutatis mutandis*, could be used here against the view (expressed by Lewis, *Analysis of Knowledge and Valuation*, p. 162, middle paragraph) that the *concept* of space suffices, if we assume, with Kant, that mathematics is knowledge of something real.

29. There is still another argument in the *Critique* (A 245; omitted from B) against the definability of categories, to wit, that such definitions are circular. I do not think the argument is valid; but inasmuch as it applies, if at all, to the pure as well as to the schematized categories, it is not relevant to our purposes here.

30. *Critique of Pure Reason*, A 729=B 758.

31. "Kant scheint bei der Einteilung der Urteile in analytisch and synthetisch von der Fiktion auszugehen, daß auch die nichtmathematischen Begriffe definiert werden können" (K. Marc-Wogau, "Kants Lehre vom analytischen Urteil," *Theoria*, XVII [1951], 150).

32. Lewis, *Analysis of Knowledge and Valuation*, p. 162.

33. *Prolegomena*, §2 c 2 (Academy edn., IV, 268; trans. Beck, p. 15)=*Critique of Pure Reason*, B 14.

34. *Prize Essay*, Academy edn., II, 277; *Über eine Entdeckung*, Academy edn., VIII, 229-31; *Critique of Pure Reason*, A 730=B 758.

35. Kant says that mathematical definitions are *willkürlich*, which is usually translated as "arbitrary." But the connotation of "random" present in "arbitrary" is not present in Kant's word "arbitrary," for Kant makes the antonym of "arbitrary" not "necessary" but "empirical" (*Lectures on Logic*, §103, Note). *Willkürlich* has reference to the volitional character of a synthetic definition, a rule for the synthesis of a concept; but a

mathematical concept is synthesized only under given conditions of intuition, and is therefore not arbitrary in the modern sense of this word.

36. *Critique of Pure Reason*, B 17=*Prolegomena*, §2 c 2.

37. *Prolegomena*, §2 c 2; *Critique of Practical Reason*, Academy edn., V, 51.

38. [This essay originally appeared in *Kant-Studien* 47 (1955), pp. 168-181, and is reprinted with permission.]

Kant's Theory of Definition

I

In most contemporary writings on the distinction between analytic and synthetic propositions, an analytic proposition is defined as one that follows from an explicit definition by rules of formal logic. If, as is usual, it is assumed that all definitions are nominal or stipulative, and further that all a priori propositions are analytic, it follows that the necessity of an a priori proposition is linguistic in origin and scope.

The original distinction between analytic and synthetic propositions, however, was drawn by Kant, who did not make any of these three assumptions. Confusion arises through discussing, in Kantian terms, a distinction whose modern usage differs widely from that of the author of the distinction; discords are produced by Kantian tones in otherwise empiricistic harmonies. Sometimes one or more of the three doctrines mentioned above is attributed to Kant himself,[1] or more often it is argued that the Kantian doctrine is important and plausible only when seen as anticipating and preparing the way for the more recent doctrines. Either of these tactics keeps Kant's own doctrines from teaching us anything important and distinctive by obscuring what was unique and original in them but has since been forgotten or neglected.

My purpose here is to try to show the relationship between Kant's own views of definition and of analytic judgment. I shall suggest that the interpretation of his analytic judgments as those based upon definitions is without historical warrant. This raises the question whether modern disputes about the possibility of a priori synthetic propositions, in which the theory of definition plays a decisive role in the formation of criteria for analyticity, are really discussions of the problem to which Kant devoted the first *Critique*.

II

To define, according to Kant, means to present the complete concept of a thing within its limits and in its primary or original character. A complete concept is one with a sufficiency of clear predicates for the entire concept to be distinct; and the predicates stated are primary or original in the sense that they are not derived from other predicates included in the definition. The predicates must, in other words, be primitive and coordinate; no derivative and subordinate predicates are admissible in a definition, for otherwise the definition would require proof.[2] If a definition does incorrectly contain derivative predicates—properties instead of *essentialia*—it is lacking in *precision*. Definition is a "sufficiently distinct and precise concept (*conceptus rei adaequatus in minimis terminis, complete determinatus*)."[3]

The definition of "definition" that Kant gives here leads him to deny the name "definition" to many sentences commonly so called. It is reached partly by an analysis of usage, and partly by a decision which makes the concept more precise: "There are definitions of concepts which we already have but which are not correctly named. In these cases, it is not that the meaning of a word is analyzed, but that a concept, which we already possess, is analyzed; and then it must be particularly shown what name properly expresses it."[4]

Kant distinguishes two major and independent divisions of definitions: into analytic and synthetic, and into nominal and real.

A definition is analytic if it is of a given concept; synthetic if of a concept made or synthesized by the definition itself.[5] The former makes a concept distinct, the latter makes a distinct concept.[6] Under each of these major divisions, there is a subdivision: the concept defined may be given or made a priori or a posteriori.[7]

An analytic definition states the original analytic predicates of the thing defined. An analytic predicate is a partial concept of a thing actually thought in the concept of the *definiendum*.[8] Thus an analytic definition is an analytic judgment containing no subordinate predicates. A synthetic definition, however, contains synthetic predicates, predicates whose union first establishes a distinct concept of the *definiendum*.

The other major division is between nominal and real definition. Kant does not draw this distinction as one between the definition of a word and the definition of a thing; because he regarded the concept, rather than thing or word, as the *definiendum* he was prevented from using this formula of the distinction. Rather the difference lies in the content of the *definiens* and in the methodological function of the two kinds of definition. A nominal definition states the logical essence of the concept of the thing, or serves merely to distinguish this thing from others. If it does only the latter, it is called a diagnostic definition in contrast to a definition stating essential primitive predicates.[9] The logical essence, stated in nominal definition, is the original primitive concept of all the *essentialia*;[10] the diagnostic definition may state only the irreducible minimum of some easily recognized attributes or properties, sufficient as a criterion in a dichotomous classification by a pass-fail test.

A real definition not only puts one word in place of others, but the *definiens* contains a clear mark by which the object can be recognized and by virtue of which the defined concept is shown to have "objective reality"—by which it is shown that there is a defined thing.[11] (The diagnostic definition does this, but not by stating the diagnostic symptom as an *essentia* of the thing.) Real definition, therefore, is a part and not merely a tool of knowledge. Real definition states the real essence constituted by real predicates, not merely by logical predicates included ("already thought in") the concept of a the subject.

A synthetic predicate is a determination (*Bestimmung*) not contained in the subject-concept but enlarging it; it is not found by analysis. It determines a thing, not merely its concept.

Anything we please can be made to serve as a logical predicate; the subject can even be predicated of itself; for logic abstracts from all content. But a *determining* predicate is a predicate which is added to the concept of the subject and enlarges it. Consequently it must not be already contained in the concept.[12]

A real definition, therefore, is always a synthetic judgment, even though the real definition, *as definition*, may be analytical and is analytical if the concept is given.[13]

Real predicates are never arbitrarily synthesized into a logical product called the essence; in every case the determinations are not purely conceptual but intuitive representations. General logic is concerned only with the logical essence or predicates; or, rather, in abstracting from all contents it treats determinations as if they were logical predicates. But knowledge of things requires knowledge of and through determinations, not merely the mouthing of their names, and this knowledge is knowledge of the real possibility of the object through a specific determination as both its *ratio essendi* and *ratio cognoscendi*.[14] We find the logical essence by reflecting on the predicates which constitute or are made to constitute the nominal definition; for real essence, we seek data from experience or intuition to determine whether and under what condition the object is really possible.[15]

This difficult and obscure matter is involved in the distinction between general and transcendental logic, and it cannot be made intelligible within the limits usually imposed on discussions of definition in formal logic. Kant is saying that in a real definition we do not merely equate a word with a logical product of arbitrarily chosen logical predicates, but we make at least a problematical existential judgment and state the conditions under which this judgment could be verified so that the *definiendum* will be seen to have "objective reference." There must be, in the *definiens*, some determination or compound of determinations that can be "cashed" in possible sensible (intuitive) experience. Its absence is the reason why all definitions in speculative metaphysics are only nominal. Its specific epistemological character is the reason also why general logic does not deal with (or at least does not distinguish) real definitions, since general logic disregards the transcendental difference between a predicate and a determination; and neglect of this difference is, finally, the reason why logic, when used as an organon in metaphysics, develops into dialectic.

The notion of real definition is not only excluded from general logic by Kant (though he dealt with it in his *Lectures on Logic*, which far exceeded the bounds he set up around the field of general logic), but is challenged on other grounds by most modern writers who reject the ontological distinction between essence and property.[16] They admit, in any specific case, the distinction between an essential and an accidental definition, though on pragmatic not ontological grounds. Kant, in accordance with a tradition going back at least to the *Port-Royal Logic*,[17] uses the distinction between nominal and real definition to designate this other, quite different, distinction: a real definition is one from which other properties can be derived, while a nominal definition suffices only for "comparisons" and not for "derivations." Thus "The circle is a curved line all of whose parts can be made to coincide" is described by Kant as a nominal definition despite the fact that it prescribes an applicable test; he means that it is a definition that contains a predicate already derived, not an *essentia*; but instead of pointing this out, he calls it nominal.[18]

Having now set up the major divisions, I turn to the specific types of definitions resulting from the two independent divisions. They may be most easily seen from the following table.

	Analytic		*Synthetic*	
NOMINAL	LOGICAL DEFINITION		DECLARATION	
REAL	A priori Exposition	A posteriori Description	A priori Construction	A posteriori Invention

I) *Analytic nominal definition.* Kant says little about this, and even that little is confusing. Because it is in any case of small importance to our inquiry, I shall not undertake to examine the various confusing statements he makes, but merely list the passages for the interested reader.[19]

2) *Synthetic nominal definition.* Such a definition is a stipulation or a "declaration" of an intended usage, the concept being created by the definition. Since they are not determined by experience or by analysis of a given concept, Kant says that such definitions are a priori synthetic, not realizing, perhaps, the inappropriateness of this adjective to what is not a proposition or judgment proper.[20]

3) *Analytic real definition.* A definition of this type states the defining predicates of a given concept known to have objective validity, and it contains the synthetic predicate (*Bestimmung*) which gives the defined concept this objective reference. Nevertheless, upon investigation it turns out that any attempt to state such a definition fails to meet the formal requirements of definition, with respect either to completeness or precision.

If the concept is given a priori, we cannot be sure that we have a complete analysis of it into its coordinate predicates. A concept given a priori may include "many obscure representations, which we overlook in our analysis, although we are constantly making use of them in our application of the concept." Therefore the completeness of a proffered definition is never more than probable, and rather than call such an indefinite analysis by the name "definition," Kant calls it an "exposition."[21]

If the concept is given a posteriori, its analysis suffers from the same infirmity mentioned above in discussing the definition of an a priori concept. Such a concept has no precise and complete analysis, for the concept itself is not a fixed union of predicates. It is variable, depending upon the scope of the experience we classify under it. Kant in one place says that it cannot even be nominally defined.[22] A statement of the attributes and properties of a thing meant by an empirical concept is at most a description, which is not held to rules of precision and completeness; description provides many truths which serve as the "material for definition,"[23] the definition itself being only an ideal.

4) *Synthetic real definition.* It is obvious from the very name what falls here: such a definition must not only make a concept, but must show its real possibility by including the *Bestimmung* which is its *ratio essendi* and *cognoscendi.*

If the synthesis is of pure concepts, the real determination must be a character of pure intuition; if of empirical concepts, the real determination must be an empirical intuition. The synthesis of pure concepts is a construction. Construction is the presentation of a concept through the spontaneous production of its corresponding and verifying intuition. Concepts, if pure, can have an a priori representation only in pure intuition; and such representation is definition as this occurs in mathematics. If the concept is empirical in its components, we have the presentation of an actual empirical intuition not through the productive imagination alone but through a change effected in the real world. A definition of such a concept may be genetic, telling us how to make a corresponding object,[24] and the devising of the object is proof that the concept has real objective possibility and is not chimerical. Kant calls such a definition (as of a ship's chronometer) a "declaration of a project"[25] or an "exposition of appearances."[26] Since "exposition" and "declaration" are both used in other senses, I have called this, in the table, "invention."

In mathematics, we make a concept by synthesis. "The mathematician in his definitions says, *Sic volo, sic jubeo.*"[27] But in spite of the modern sound of this statement, mathematical definitions for Kant are real, not nominal. Mathematical entities are not arbitrary logical products of compatible logical predicates; the concepts have objective validity (in pure intuition) shown through the presentation of the corresponding determination. If the presentation is a product of the productive imagination, the construction is called schematic or pure, as of a figure (no matter how roughly drawn) used in a geometrical proof. Such a figure is not used empirically, and the actual drawing of it is not a part of the science of mathematics but belongs to art. Kant calls the empirically made sketch "technical construction"[28] and, indeed, it is like the "invention" of any empirical object. Mathematics is the only science able to construct its concepts a priori, and only by construction can we achieve completeness and precision in knowledge. Therefore mathematics is the only science which contains proper and strict definitions.[29]

Kant often speaks of synthetic definitions, including mathematical definitions, as *willkürlich.* The word *willkürlich*, ordinarily translated as "arbitrary," does not, however, suggest the caprice sometimes understood in the word "arbitrary"; "arbitrary" does not mean "random." Arbitrariness, as it is now commonly interpreted, is not a feature of mathematical knowledge as Kant interprets it; mathematical concepts are limited by the fixed conditions of intuition, just as empirical concepts are synthesized under the limits imposed by the actual content and order of empirical data. Kant contrasts *willkürlich* with *empirisch*, not, I think, with *notwendig*.[30]

III

I shall now consider the role that definitions play in the progress of knowledge, as this is described by Kant.

The search for definitions of empirical concepts is justified by the technical demands for communication in relatively unambiguous language. We need to "fix" the meaning of a concept from time to time, and we do so by nominal definition or declaration. Such definitions, if made too soon or especially if taken too seriously as a part rather than as an instrument of knowledge, distort inquiry by permitting logical analysis to usurp the place of empirical amplification. "What useful purpose," Kant asks, "could be served by defining an empirical concept, such, for instance, as that of water? When we speak of water and its properties, we do not stop short at what is thought in the word 'water' but proceed to experiments."[31] Description suffices; definition which aims at being more than nominal is a useless presumption.

Turning from empirical to rational knowledge, Kant insists upon a sharp distinction between the methods proper to mathematics and those of philosophy. The mathematician begins with definitions and proceeds by a synthetic method (involving constructions) to his conclusions; his definitions cannot be false, and their only fault may be lack of precision, which is progressively corrected.[32] The philosopher, on the other hand, must begin with concepts already given to him, though confusedly and without sufficient determinateness. The thing meant is not intuitively clear in the sign, as in the concepts of mathematics,[33] all of which are subject to construction in intuition. The symbols, such as a set of points representing a number, have their meaning "on their face"; whereas the philosopher must use his symbols only as poor representations of richer concepts. These he must analyze in order to compare their segregated characteristics with those originally intended by a ready-made concept used to render unanalyzed experience intelligible. A definition reached by synthesis in philosophy could only by accident be a definition of a concept which originally posed the philosophical problem to us.

In mathematics there are few unanalyzable concepts, and they can be used with assurance according to explicit rules without any need for analysis. Analyses of concepts, if made at all, belong to the philosophy of mathematics rather than to mathematics itself. In philosophy, on the contrary, there are many unanalyzable and indefinable concepts, but we do not begin our work with them. We discover what they are only by the analysis of given concepts, which are not entirely clear and distinct. Thus (if he is fortunate) the philosopher ends where the mathematician begins, to wit, with indefinable elementary concepts and definitions of the concepts given in the beginning. Definitions in philosophy, therefore, are not the conditions of knowledge; they are what we hope to conclude with, not the raw material with which we begin.

From these textual inquiries, we can conclude that definition does not play the dominant role in Kant's philosophy that it does in later theories of analytic judgment. In only one field, mathematics, does Kant admit strict definitions, and in mathematics it is possible to decide indubitably what is analytic and what is synthetic. In empirical knowledge, definition is only loose and informal, and we should expect what we do find, namely that decision on the character of specific judgments is variable and without great importance. It is a priori judgments outside of mathematics that Kant is chiefly concerned to establish, and of their concepts definition is impossible. Yet it is with respect to these judgments that it is of fundamental importance to distinguish the apriority of formal logic (analytic) from the apriority of transcendental logic (synthetic).

Definition is not essential to certainty in knowledge. Quite apart from Kant's belief that not all a priori knowledge is analytic, he does not even assert that analytic judgments are necessarily consequences of definitions. Though he indicates[34] that analytic judgments are deducible from definitions, this statement occurs in the reply to Eberhard, in a context supplied by his opponent; it is not his characteristic way of stating the nature of analytic judgments. Definition would be a sufficient, but is not a necessary, condition for analytic judgments; we may have a priori knowledge of undefined concepts provided we can either exhibit the concept in pure intuition (schematize it to give a basis for synthetic judgments) or give a partial analysis of the concept.[35] And in three places,[36] at least, Kant describes the way logical certainty in knowledge is gained, showing clearly that definition is given a secondary role. He tells us that we begin by analyzing concepts, expressing the analyses in analytic judgments, and only then organize these analytic judgments into definitions. Even so, definition requires a completeness and precision that is often an unattainable ideal; yet its absence does not jeopardize the analytic judgments already made.

The *Critique of Pure Reason* is supposed to answer the question, How are synthetic judgments a priori possible? But if it is not possible to decide objectively whether a given judgment is synthetical or analytical, the entire *Critique* seems to be wasted effort. Can we make synthetic judgments and know that they will, as it were, remain synthetic while we examine their apriority? Or do not definitions grow and so extend their sway that a judgment once known only empirically can, under better definitions, come to be logically necessary? Can we not agree[37] that a "synthetic a priori judgment" is a judgment with an ambiguous term, and that when we remove the ambiguity by definition we either remove the apriority or the syntheticity?

This presupposes that analytic judgments are determined by definitions, and it at least suggests that definitions are arbitrary in such a manner that we have a choice as to whether the judgment in question will be made analytic or synthetic. Expressed in other ways, this is one of the oldest and probably the most common of all criticisms of Kant's theory. The difference which he thought was fundamental seems to be a subjective, shifting distinction, dependent upon how much one knows at a given time, and how one formulates what one knows. Very early in his use of the distinction Kant seems to have anticipated this objection[38] though he gave no answer at that time, and for many years used the distinction as though completely oblivious of the objection.

He does not seem to have realized its full force until he prepared his reply to Eberhard. Even then, in the published reply he does not come to grips with the problem; but in the working paper prepared under his direction by Schultz there is a passage[39] which deals with the shifting of the line between the two types of judgments by the modification of definition. The passage is obscure, but I will try to describe what I think Kant would have said had he put it into shape for publication.

Kant invites his opponent to add any attributes he wishes to a concept, so that whatever it is he wishes to prove he can prove by deduction, i.e., analytically. But then Kant asks him: How did you come to include in the concept precisely those attributes you needed in order to render previously synthetic judgments analytic? He cannot reply that he is giving a definition of the concept unless he can show that he is obeying the rules of definition in formal logic. That is, he must be able to show that the newly introduced attributes are logically independent of the old, yet invariably attached to the subject in experience, so that the conjunction of the old and new attributes has the same denotation as the original concept. A narrower denotation will not do, for that means that a new concept has been introduced, not that an old one has been defined. Now in order to know the identity of the old and new denotation, he must know the connection of the independent attributes before stating them in a new definition; he must know this synthetically, for if they are analytically related the rule concerning the precision of definition is broken. Hence, definitions devised for the purpose of rendering synthetic judgments analytic are not real definitions, or in making them we must already know with certainty the synthetic judgment they were designed to establish as analytic. If they are not real but only nominal definitions, then the problem of synthetic a priori knowledge (which Kant calls the metaphysical problem) is not touched by this exercise in logic.[40]

IV

In contrast with the views mentioned at the beginning of this paper, sometimes erroneously attributed to Kant, we have found that Kant's views on the relation between definition and analytic judgment are as follows. While a judgment logically implied by a definition is analytic, analytical judgments are not necessarily or even usually known or justified by deduction from definitions. Analytic judgments are made by analysis of concepts which need not first be established by definition. Definition is a late stage in the progress of knowledge, being preceded by the analysis of given concepts, expressed in analytic judgments. Because definition is a secondary and more or less adventitious element in Kant's theory of the criteria of analytic judgment, the view that synthetic propositions can be rendered analytic by a change in definition is foreign to the distinction as Kant established and used it, and does not contribute to a solution of his problem of justifying a priori judgments whose necessity is not that of formal logic.[41]

NOTES

1. Three widely scattered specimens are: (a) "La notion kantienne du jugement analytique semble d'exiger que les concepts soient d'une part absolument susceptibles d'une définition unique, rigoureuse et sans aucune ambiguité, et que d'un autre côté leurs définitions soient susceptible d'être analysées sans qu'on aboutisse à des jugements synthétiques" (Paul Tannery, *Bulletin de la Société Française de Philosophie* [1903], 124); (b) "Kant scheint bei der Einteilung der Urteile in analytisch and synthetisch von der Fiktion auszugehen, daß auch die nicht-mathematischen Begriffe definiert werden können" (K. Marc-Wogau, *Theoria*, XVII [1951], 150); (c) "The distinction...is easy and clear as long as we deal with merely stipulated or nominal definitions, as Kant seems to have supposed we could" (R. E. Gahringer, *Journal of Philosophy*, LI [1954], 435).

2. See *Critique of Pure Reason*, A 727=B 755 and note.

3. *Logik. Ein Handbuch zu Vorlesungen*, §99 (Academy edn., IX, 140). Hereafter cited as *Lectures on Logic*.

4. *Reflection* 3003 (Academy edn., XVI, 610).

5. *Lectures on Logic*, §100.

6. *Ibid.*, Introduction, VIII (Academy edn., IX, 63); see also *Reflection* 2929.

7. *Lectures on Logic*, §101.

8. *Ibid.*, Academy edn., IX, 59.

9. *Reflections* 2994, 3003.

10. *Lectures on Logic*, Introduction, VIII (Academy edn., IX, 61).

11. *Critique of Pure Reason*, A 241-42 n.

12. *Critique of Pure Reason*, A 598=B 626, trans. Kemp Smith; cf. *Reflection* 4055.

13. *Reflections* 2955, 2994.

14. *Lectures on Logic*, Introduction, VIII (Academy edn., IX, 61). *Ratio essendi* is, of course, to be understood not as having a bearing on the thing itself, corresponding to the "real essence" in Locke; for Kant, like Locke, admits ignorance of that. But *ratio essendi* may be applied also to the object of knowledge; and when its *ratio cognoscendi* and *ratio essendi* in part coincide, there is a priori knowledge.

15. *Critique of Pure Reason*, A 218=B 265. Kant insists on the distinction between the two meanings of possibility as early as the *Einzig möglicher Beweisgrund*...(Academy edn., II, 77-78), the most important point always being that existence is not a logical predicate. There are many things logically possible that are not really possible, because the nonconceptual condition that would show them to exist is not possible. Thus "a two-sided plane figure" is logically but not really possible, while a "two-sided triangle" is not logically possible (*Critique*, A 221=B 268). The only kind of possibility subject to formal definition is logical (*Critique*, A 244=B 302).

16. See Richard Robinson, *Definition* (New York: Oxford University Press, 1950), pp. 154-55.

17. Arnauld, *Port-Royal Logic*, Part I, ch. 12.

18. *Reflection* 2916; see also *Reflection* 2995. He does, however, point out the real infirmity of this definition in the *Critique*, A 732=B 760.

19. *Lectures on Logic*, §106, Note 2; *Reflections* 2918, 2931, 2963, 3004.

20. *Reflection* 3007. Such a definition—in the case under discussion, it happens to be Kant's definition of analytic judgment—cannot be in error. See *Über eine Entdeckung...*, Academy edn., VIII, 232.

21. *Critique of Pure Reason*, A 728-29=B 756-57, trans. Kemp Smith.

22. *Reflection* 2992.

23. *Lectures on Logic*, §105, Note 3 (Academy edn., IX, 143).

24. See *Reflection* 3001.

25. *Critique of Pure Reason*, A 729=B 757.

26. *Lectures on Logic*, §102.

27. *Reflection* 2930 (Academy edn., XVI, 579); see also *Inquiry on the Distinctness of the Principles of Natural Theology and Morals* (hereafter referred to as *Prize Essay*), Academy edn., II, §1 (trans. L. W. Beck, in *Kant's Critique of Practical Reason and other Writings in Moral Philosophy*, p. 262).

28. *Über eine Entdeckung*, Academy edn., VIII, 192 n.

29. *Critique of Pure Reason*, A 729=B 757.

30. *Lectures on Logic*, §103, Note.

31. *Critique of Pure Reason*, A 728=B 756, trans. Kemp Smith.

32. *Reflection* 2979.

33. See *Critique of Pure Reason*, A 734=B 762; *Prize Essay*, Academy edn., II, 278.

34. *Über eine Entdeckung*, Academy edn., VIII, 229.

35. *Critique of Pure Reason*, A 731=B 759; *Prize Essay*, Academy edn., II, 285; *Lectures on Logic*, §109, Note (Academy edn., IX, 145).

36. *Prize Essay*, Academy edn., II, 282; *The False Subtlety of the Four Syllogistic Figures*, Academy edn., II, 61; *Prolegomena*, §2 c 3 (Academy edn., IV, 273).

37. With H. W. Chapman, *Mind*, N.S., LXI (1952), 391.

38. *Reflection* 3928, dating from the late 1760's.

39. *Rezension von Eberhards Magazin*, Academy edn., XX, 408-9.

40. I have translated this passage and discussed the issue of the variability of the synthetic-analytic decision in "Can Kant's Synthetic Judgments Be Made Analytic?", [included in this volume, pp. 1-15 above].

41. [This essay originally appeared in *The Philosophical Review* 65 (1956), pp. 179-91, copyright 1956 by Cornell University, and is reprinted with permission.]

Apodictic Imperatives

RELATION AND MODALITY OF IMPERATIVES

At the end of §1 of the *Critique of Practical Reason* there is an extraordinary statement in which Kant distinguishes between the practical rightness and the categoricalness of an imperative, and indicates that the former might be independent of the latter. This is astonishing, because the reader has been led, in the *Foundations,* to believe that by establishing a categorical imperative a moral imperative is established. But Kant, in discussing the example, "Never make a deceitful promise," says: "If, now, it is found that this rule is practically right, it is a law, because it is a categorical imperative."

Though Kant says in the *Foundations* that there is only one categorical imperative, from time to time he calls specific imperatives to do certain actions categorical imperatives. For instance, in the *Metaphysics of Morals*, "Obey authority" is called a categorical imperative.[1] I do not know of any instance in which Kant calls an imperative "categorical" and does not regard it as "practically right." But there are indeed imperatives which are formally categorical and yet not "practically right." There are likewise hypothetical imperatives which are morally binding and hence practically right. "Shut the door" is formally categorical, while "If you are married, remain faithful to your spouse" is formally hypothetical. Presumably it would be possible to show that the latter is "practically right" and is in some sense a law.[2] And certainly the former is not "practically right" in the sense required if we are to regard it as a law; it is at most technically practical and not morally practical.[3]

It is clear from these examples that the term "categorical" in Kant's ordinary usage of "categorical imperative" does more than refer to the form of the imperative. And it is worth noting that the distinction among imperatives, when first introduced in the *Foundations*, is not based on a difference in form of the imperatives themselves, but on their ways of commanding: "All imperatives command either hypothetically or categorically."[4] The distinction between hypothetical and categorical imperatives, which seems to be a formal distinction, is derivative from this prior distinction, which is modal.

What is involved in being "practically right" is not the category of relation, but the category of modality. The best name for what Kant called the "categorical imperative" and identified with the "imperative of morality" would seem to be "apodictic imperative." In the *Foundations* and occasionally in the second *Critique,* terms of modality are used to distinguish among the several imperatives. The technical imperative is called problematic, the pragmatic is called assertoric, and the categorical is called apodictic. But in general the modal division is neglected in favor of the formal. Whereas Paton expresses a certain distrust of the modal division,[5] the purpose of this paper is to justify its use by drawing attention to certain considerations which are neglected as a result of Kant's insistence upon the formal or relational distinction.

The "Table of the Categories of Freedom" in the *Critique of Practical Reason* is regrettably of no help to us in deciding on the propriety of the term "apodictic imperative." This Table is, I may venture to say, one of Kant's less successful productions in the architectonic *genre,* and it is hard to make heads or tails of it, especially in its division of moments under the dynamical categories.[6] The distinction between hypothetical and categorical does not appear under "Relation." Under "Modality," corresponding to the moments of necessity and contingency there is "Perfect and Imperfect Duty," while "Duty" itself appears as the member corresponding to the assertoric judgment of existence. According to this Table, an "apodictic imperative" would be an imperative of strict or perfect duty, commanding without exception a definite action (e.g., paying a debt); such imperatives belong to jurisprudence, not to ethics, because they command a specific action without concern with the motive.[7] The contrary of an apodictic imperative is not a prohibition[8] but the imperative of imperfect duty. Such an imperative is not a command to do a certain action, but to act on a certain motive, with room left for the determination of the occasion and the specific kind and direction of the action. Imperatives of imperfect duty belong only to ethics and not to jurisprudence.

In this essay I propose to use the name "apodictic imperative" for all moral imperatives whether they allow *latitudo*[9] in action or not. Imperatives which are not apodictic or necessary will be treated as imperatives which carry no moral weight, according to Kant's estimate. They correspond to the first category of modality in the Table in the *Critique of Practical Reason* and not to the second, which already introduces the concept of duty. But they correspond, in their two species, to the problematic and assertoric modalities in the Table of judgments of the first *Critique.*

There are two textual justifications for this, apart from the negative justification of the obscurity of the Table itself. The first is that moral imperatives, whether strict or loose, are necessary—the strict necessitating a specific action, the loose necessitating a general maxim and rendering it a law which yet permits "variety in the rule."[10] As necessary, they are products of reason, which (in its logical use) is the faculty of apodictic knowledge.[11] And, more importantly, we have seen that Kant himself on occasion calls them apodictic imperatives.

ANALYSIS OF HYPOTHETICAL IMPERATIVES OF THE FIRST TYPE

A hypothetical (problematic or assertoric) imperative is one which holds for any rational being under the condition that this being has a certain end or purpose which is believed to be the effect of the action he is told to execute, and which states this condition as the restrictive condition on the validity of the imperative. We shall call these imperatives *conditional imperatives* or *hypothetical imperatives of the first type,* and under them are included two modal types: assertoric and the problematic imperatives.

A full analysis of such an imperative would make the following components explicit:

a) In the protasis:
　　1)A conative element: an incentive, impulse, or interest in something (*B*), which is the purpose of the commanded action; an object or state of affairs the representation of which is one of the causes of its existence through the relation of the representation to the overt action of the subject; expressed in the imperative as "If I want *B*" or "Because I want *B*."
　　2)A cognitive element: knowledge of the causal relation between the action commanded (*A*) and the purpose or end *(B);* equivalent under condition (1), to "*A* is a means to *B*."
　　3)A logical form: "If I fully will the effect [*B*], I must also will the action [*A*] necessary to it."[12]
b) The apodosis: "Do *A*."

In the technical imperative or rule of skill, the fully expanded form woulḋ be: "(1) If you will *B*, (2) because *A* is a necessary condition of *B*, then by (3) do *A*." Here the problematic element lies in the first conditional: "if you will *B*...." *If A* is really commanded under this condition, (2) must here be assertoric.[13] In the pragmatic imperative or counsel of prudence, the full exposition would be: "Because you will *B* (*B*=happiness), *(2)* if *A* is a necessary condition of *B*, then by (3) do *A*." Here the problematic element lies not in the antecedent conation, since a rational being having any desires necessarily desires his happiness;[14] it lies in our irremediable uncertainty as to what is the empirical content of *B* and whether *A* will in fact lead to it.

Kant tells us that the possibility of these imperatives is easy to establish, because they are, in what concerns the will, analytic.[15] This is correct,[16] but it requires a little attention to see what it means and why it is true.

It is not entirely clear in what sense an imperative can be either analytic or synthetic. Imperatives are not judgments with a subject and predicate, and so do not fall under Kant's explicit division of the types of judgment. And though for any imperative a set of indicative (but not necessarily factual)[17] statements may be formulated under which the imperative could be derived by a syntactical change of mood, in the case of hypothetical imperatives of the first type, some of the corresponding judgments are themselves hypothetical, and hence likewise fall outside Kant's official rubric for distinguishing analytic from synthetic judgments. It is not entirely pedantic to insist on these points; but the minor infelicities of expression should not permit us to overlook the important point Kant is insisting upon, even though he does it in not entirely suitable language. I shall try to say, therefore, what I think he means.

If we take the statements of the conditions under which the apodosis is regarded as binding and phrase them in declarative statements, e.g., "Under conditions *C* a rational being will choose *A*," then the proposition "A rational being will choose *A*" will follow analytically from this and the proposition, "A rational being is under conditions *C*." By "following analytically" I mean that a denial of the conclusion will contradict a premise. Thus: "If a rational being fully wills *B* and knows *A* to be a necessary condition of *B*, and if (3) to will fully an end includes willing the means known to be necessary to this end, then the rational being wills *A*," is analytic in the broad sense in which Kant *here* uses the word "analytic," since to deny the apodosis is to contradict the protasis. But it is not analytic in the strict Kantian sense, since an analytic proposition for Kant is one whose denial is self-contradictory, and the mere concept of rational being does not analytically "contain" the concept of willing *A*.

But it is analytic, even in the broad sense, only in what concerns the will. That *A* is necessary to *B* is not known analytically, and that the rational being in fact wills *B* (except perhaps when *B*=happiness) is likewise not known analytically. All that is known analytically is (3), and this concerns the form of volition and not the contents willed. (3) is not actually a premise,[18] but a rule of practical inference, specifying the relation between the variables *A* and *B*. Kant should say, therefore, not that the hypothetical imperatives of the first type are analytic, but that their formal principle, (3), is analytic. "If you wish to have bread, devise a mill" is not, fortunately for most of us, in any sense analytic, but is only a disguised form of the empirical statement, "Mills grind flour, and flour is needed to make bread."

I shall call (3) the formal principle of hypothetical imperatives of the first type.[19] It is indeed analytical, and it alone concerns the will independently of the cognitive content and contingencies of human desire. Not to accept (3) is to fail to be a rational being concerned with desires. It is for this reason that Kant holds even hypothetical imperatives of this type to be objectively valid; they are not persuasive or emotive but rational, even though they are relevant to action only under specific conditions which are not true of rational beings as such; and the conditions they are concerned with are conditions of him to whom the imperative is directed, not of him who issues the command.

Since beings like men do not, in fact, always will the means necessary to their ends, even when they do know the means, the hypothetical imperative of this type expresses a constraint. If we were completely rational beings, the maxim of doing whatever is necessary to the end in view would be easy to follow; but since we are not completely rational, even our desires and wishes create constraints and not mere lures and enticements.

ANALYSIS OF CATEGORICAL IMPERATIVES
OF THE FIRST TYPE

By a categorical imperative of the first type I refer to the only kind of "imperative of morality" to which Kant devoted his attention. I mean what Kant himself ordinarily called categorical imperatives.

Syntactically, the so-called categorical imperative is atomic and has no analysis. "Shut the door" is a categorical imperative which means —Shut the door. A genetic account of its utterance can be given, but the reasons for it are not even implicit in the sentence. From the sentence, we cannot reconstruct the reasons for it. There are indeed reasons for the utterance, but they are not stated as conditions under which it is imperative that the door be shut. The imperative may be honored for these or for other reasons, or rejected in spite of them without any contradiction occurring.

Obviously this is not what Kant means by "categorical imperative." He means one which not only fails to mention the conditions, but one which is independent of conditions which could be stated only in the protasis of a hypothetical imperative and which would concern only our private wants. As to the conative component, the categorical imperative is independent of any "material of desire" or "object of interest," even though they are present in every volition.[20] As to the cognitive component, it is not a condition for the imperative since the imperative does not command us to do anything as a means to an end; indeed, it may not command us to *do* anything, but only to will to do something in a certain way.[21] And as to the third condition, the formal principle does not have the right "logical shape" for an unconditional imperative, since we are not concerned with connecting a variable in (1) with a variable in (2).

Hence it is necessary to look elsewhere than to an analysis of the categorical imperative in order to discover whether it is "objectively right and hence a law."

Whereas Kant told us that the hypothetical imperative was analytic and hence easy to establish, he called the categorical imperative "an a priori synthetic proposition"; "it connects [the willing of an action] directly with the concept of the will of a rational being as something which is not contained within it."[22] That which would be "contained within it" would be the concept of an object of desire as contained in the concept of the will of a sensuous being like man. The imperative which would follow analytically from such a synthetical concept (the concept of will modified by an accident) would, of course, be a hypothetical imperative of the first type, conditional upon the empirical character of the specific desires of a finite being with an empirically restricted will.

Yet Kant says immediately thereafter that "the mere concept of a categorical imperative" furnishes "the formula containing the only proposition that can be a categorical imperative." He then goes on to point out the fact which chiefly concerns us in the present essay: to know the formula of a categorical imperative and to know how it is practically right as a law are two very different things. This paragraph contains a number of notions that are a bit obscure, and we must attempt to clarify them.

Kant tells us that the mere concept of a categorical imperative furnishes the formula containing the proposition which can be a categorical imperative. Yet, two paragraphs later, he does not give us what he calls a "formula" but what he calls *the one* "categorical imperative." It is, in fact, a categorical imperative; but the words "maxim" and "law" in it are variables, and it really does state a formula. Broad is correct in calling it "the supreme principle of all categorical imperatives" and in referring to it as a "second-order principle," the first-order principle being a specific imperative fitting this formula.[23]

"Do X" might in one sense be considered a formula for the categorical imperative; but this is not what Kant means by a formula. A formula, he says, determines what is to be done in solving a problem,[24] and "Do X" does not help us in determining the permissible range of values of "X." We must find a formula from which the values of "X" can be determined, independently of any protasis such as (a1) and (a2), since they are not stated in a categorical imperative.

There seems, at first sight, to be a contradiction in saying that the mere concept of a categorical imperative implies its formula, and in saying that the imperative (or rather its formula, which is the implicate) is synthetic. But it is not really so, at least in Kantian terminology. For him, a proposition which is itself synthetic can be proved analytically; for him, "analytic" is not equivalent to "logically deducible." Mathematical propositions, he at least sometimes says,[25] are synthetical propositions, but can be proved by analysis of synthetic a priori propositions. To be analytical, the contradictory of a proposition must be self-contradictory, and not merely contradictory of some other propositions used in its proof.[26] Hence it is quite possible for Kant to say that the formula follows by analysis of the concept of a categorical imperative, and to say that it is not analytical of any concept contained within it.

Finally, there is the danger we have already noticed in saying that an imperative is *either* analytic *or synthetic*. But if we remember that an imperative is only the mood in which a law is formulated for a being who ought to but does not by nature do what the law says a rational being would do,[27] we can easily enough formulate the law to which the imperative corresponds, and it is this law that Kant means is synthetic. Unfortunately, however, after carefully distinguishing "law" from "imperative" he fails to remain faithful to his distinction, and says many things about imperatives that can correctly be said only about laws.

All laws are synthetic judgments, and if they are laws in a strict sense (whether laws of nature or laws of morality) they are, for Kant, a priori.[28] This is true of the laws which are component (a2) in hypothetical imperatives of the first type, though usually we have to be content, in that position, to make do with merely empirical generalizations. The law which the moral imperative expresses, which is the moral law, does not occupy a position in relation to the categorical imperative comparable to that of (a2) in relation to the hypothetical. The moral law functions more like the principle (a3), with the categorical imperative (or rather *its* formula) being an immediate inference with a change of mood from this law. Factors like (a1) and (a2) do not function in the determination of the formula, but provide only the variety, content, and occasion of specific first-order categorical imperatives ("rules") under the general formula or principle.

We are now prepared to trace Kant's derivation of the formula of a categorical imperative from the concept of a categorical imperative.

For there to be any imperative which is not merely an unreasoned ejacula-
tion in the imperative mood, there must be a law. The imperative expresses the
necessitation of an action, the necessity (either conditional or unconditional) of
which is expressed in a natural law. Unless there were such a law, imperatives
would be mere prayers or persuasions or ejaculations for which no reason could
be given. Even "Shut the door" is a reasonable command only if there is some
natural law, or at least an empirical generalization, relating events like shutting
the door to other events of a desired kind. Only where there is a law can the distinction be drawn between valid and invalid imperatives, even on the assertoric
and problematical levels.

In a categorical imperative, however, the imperative is not explicitly restricted to any condition such as (a1), and therefore it cannot be the content of a
law (a2), as a law of nature, which determines the content of the imperative, i.e.,
the specific value of the variable "A" which is to be done. For if (a1) is not
specified as the condition of the imperative, there is no ground on which a specific law under *(a2)* can be chosen from all the known laws of nature to give a
specific value to this variable. For the content of any specific law that is used in
formulating a categorical imperative that is not an unreasoned and indefensible
command ("*Sic volo, sic jubeo!*") we must substitute the form of a law, and require that that form be a restrictive condition upon the maxim of action, and not
require that the content of a natural law (which is not given) be a restrictive condition upon the content of the maxim. That is to say, the categorical imperative
commands that the maxim *itself* have the form of universal and necessary law.
This form alone must determine the content of the maxim.

Now this determination of the content of a maxim by its form is just what
most critics of Kant deny is possible. I believe that this objection is based
upon—not a profound misunderstanding but—a simple misunderstanding of
what Kant is about. What he is establishing, as we have said, is a principle of
categorical imperatives, a formula, a second-order principle, and not an imperative for a specific action. The content of the maxim which is derived from its
form is the maxim to act only on maxims that fit the formula; but what these
maxims are is not determined, with respect to *their* content, by the formula. The
maxims which in fact fit under the formula will have their content determined
by considerations of type (a1) and (a2); otherwise the action would have no
specificity or overt quality. But the form of universal law serves, in the formula,
to determine the second-order maxim, which is the maxim to follow maxims
which allow universalization, and to follow them *because* they are universalizable.

It is necessary here to distinguish between the categorical imperative itself
and the formula of the categorical imperative. The former is an order to do actions of a certain kind, e.g., to let no offense pass unavenged, to treat others
fairly, to preserve one's own life, etc. The latter is an order which tells us to
choose among these maxims by a certain criterion, to wit, that the accepted
maxim be one that at the same time we can will to be a maxim for all rational

beings. What Kant ordinarily calls categorical imperatives, such as "Do not make a deceitful promise" and "Obey authority" are imperatives which have passed the criterion of the formula, and they are "practically right." It is these which I call "categorical imperatives of the first type." Categorical imperatives of the second type are those imperatives in the form "Do *A*" which do not fit under the formula. The categorical imperative—if there is such an imperative which is neither an unreasoned and indefensible command nor an elliptical formulation of a hypothetical imperative—must be to act only on a maxim that can be willed at the same time (i.e., by the very same decision to obey) to be a maxim (i.e., a law) for all rational beings.

A categorical imperative which is "practically right" must be one that commands an action which is motivated by a maxim that fits the formula. Many imperatives of the form "Do *A*" fail to meet this test. And a man may act on what is, in fact, a maxim that fits this formula, and yet do it without having his action determined by the formula. In this event, his action is legal, but not strictly moral. To show that a maxim to follow the formula can actually be an effective factor in the choice of maxims or imperatives of the first order is the task of showing that the moral imperative is "possible."

DEDUCTION OF THE CATEGORICAL IMPERATIVE
OF THE FIRST TYPE

We have seen that Kant distinguishes between establishing the formula of a categorical imperative—the process we have just traced—from learning how such a law is "possible." To show that a principle is possible is not, for Kant, to show that it is logically possible, i.e., not self-contradictory. It is not even to show that it is "really possible," but to show that it is necessary. "Necessary" in this sense is modal, not logical, for only analytic propositions have logical necessity. Real necessity means "necessity for possible experience," and is shown only by a transcendental deduction, a regression from an experience upon its conditions. To show that the categorical imperative is possible, therefore, is to show that the imperative "really holds" and is unconditionally binding. In the case before us, it is to show that it is "practically right."

Kant says that, in one sense, this deduction cannot be accomplished.[29] Yet in saying this, he is exaggerating the differences between the procedure in the theoretical and in the practical fields. The moral law, "the sole fact of pure reason,"[30] is like the laws of mathematics and natural science in Kant's theoretical philosophy. The synthetic structure of the first and second *Critiques* should not hide from us what is obvious in the analytical procedure of the *Prolegomena* and *Foundations,* namely, that morality and our knowledge of nature are the *prius,* the *explicans* and not the *explicate.* To show that a categorical imperative is really possible requires us to show:

a) That the phenomena of moral constraint are not explicable if all imperatives are conditional upon desires;[31]

b) That the world is such that the commands of the moral law or the formula of the categorical imperative, worked out analytically under (*a*), are in principle performable, i.e., that there is no reason for asserting that the moral law makes impossible demands of us, so that the phenomena of moral constraint would have to be regarded as chimerical. This is shown by the resolution of the antinomy between freedom and natural causation in the *Critique of Pure Reason*.[32]

The connection between the former, which grows out of an analysis of moral phenomena, and the latter, which is metaphysical (in the usual sense of the word) is achieved through the assimilation of the concept of autonomy, as required by genuine moral constraint, to that of freedom as a permissible consequence drawn from transcendental idealism.[33]

In one direction, the reality (binding character) of the moral law is deduced (justified) by being shown to be possible, it being already given as a fact. In the other direction, it is the reality of freedom which is justified by this fact, only the possibility of freedom having been shown in theoretical philosophy.[34]

The moral law, together with its corresponding imperative, is shown to be synthetical by showing that the mere concept of a rational will does not logically "contain" but "implies" the concept of freedom, and then by showing the law for a free agent to be self-given, i.e., a law of autonomy, expressed in an imperative not conditional upon anything except the freedom of a rational being as such. Hence it follows that a being with a will and a being who can address categorical imperatives to himself are identical, since both concepts are mediated by a "third," that of freedom.

The "Deduction" in the second *Critique* is one of the most obscure and difficult and, in one respect at least, unconvincing, parts of that work. It will not be necessary in this place to point out more than one of the difficulties, one which is characteristic of many parts of Kant's work. This is the difficulty, apparent enough to everyone except seemingly to Kant himself, of sharply distinguishing in many cases between those judgments that are analytic and those that are synthetic. Fortunately, however, the most important steps in his argument do not depend upon specific decisions, made from time to time, concerning analyticity vs. syntheticity. The important thing is not to agree with Kant concerning precisely what is "contained in" and what is only "implied by" the concept of rational being, but to see that Kant is going beyond purely formal considerations of the deduction of the formula from the concept, and is giving some existential status, in a broad sense at least, to the moral judgment. He is trying to show by a general moral, phenomenological, and philosophical consideration, that there are categorical imperatives that are morally practicable as well as logically possible.

But there is nothing in the "Deduction" that requires that the imperative which meets these requirements shall be categorical in form.

SUMMARY OF DISTINCTIONS AMONG TYPES OF IMPERATIVES

We have already seen that there are categorical imperatives which are not in fact unconditionally binding, and that there are also unconditionally binding imperatives which are not formally categorical. Those Kant is generally concerned with, however, are put forth unconditionally, in categorical form, as practically right. The various possibilities may be conveniently listed as follows:

a) Hypothetical imperatives which are conditional, i.e., either assertoric or problematic. These are the only hypothetical imperatives that Kant discusses, and are here called "hypothetical imperatives of the first type." Example: "If you want to be happy, try to develop an interest in some hobby."

b) Unconditional, i.e., apodictic, categorical imperatives; imperatives that are "practically right" in categorical form. These are the categorical imperatives Kant emphasizes, and are here called "categorical imperatives of the first type," but must be distinguished from the "*formula*" of the categorical imperatives, which apply only to this type. Example: "Obey authority."

c) Conditional categorical imperatives. These are imperatives in categorical form irrespective of whether they are "practically right" or not. They may in fact be only elliptical expressions of hypothetical imperatives, and are here called "categorical imperatives of the second type." Example: "Shut the door."

d) Unconditional hypothetical imperatives or apodictic hypothetical imperatives. These are here called "hypothetical imperatives of the second type." Example: "If you make a promise, keep it."

It will be noticed that the "first type" under each of the formal divisions is the one that Kant considered, and the "second type" is the one which he neglected.

In the next section, we shall be concerned with the distinction between (*b*) and (*c*), between categorical imperatives of the first and second types, i.e., between categorical imperatives which are apodictic and those which are not. In the final section we shall discuss the distinction between (*a*) and (*d*), between the two modalities of hypothetical imperatives.

CONDITIONAL AND UNCONDITIONAL CATEGORICAL IMPERATIVES

A recent excellent history of philosophy says: "It is possible to generalize into universal rules all sorts of maxims which nobody (and certainly not Kant) would hold to be obligatory. For instance, I could perfectly well hold that every purchaser of a new book should write his name on the flyleaf when he acquires it. There is nothing self-contradictory about this maxim."[35]

"Write your name on the flyleaf of your book" is a categorical imperative. Why is it not obligatory, and why is it an instance of (*c*) and not of (*b*)? The answer is clear from the formula, which applies to case (*b*) only (and, as we shall see, to case [*d*]). The formula is negative, telling us to act *only* according to a universalizable maxim; it expresses a necessary but not a sufficient condition for the maxim of the action. And in Kant's formula we are commanded to act only on a maxim *through which* and *at the same time* we could will that the maxim should hold for all men.[36] In Mr. Jones' example, there seem to be two separate volitions which are independent of each other, while Kant's formula is that in the very maxim of our action and *because* of it we must take account of its universalizability. The maxim holds for my own action, if it is moral, *only in so far as* I can will it to hold as a maxim for others. Any maxim that passes the test of universalization is legally permissible; there is nothing wrong or unreasonable in my willing to put my name in my books, or indeed in willing that others should do so too. But only the maxim which is a principle of action for me *because* I regard it as binding on rational beings generally is a maxim having moral status.

Under conditional categorical imperatives, therefore, we must distinguish two sub-types: (1) An imperative which, if followed universally, would bring no opposition or antagonism into the relations among personal beings—legal (i.e., legally possible) imperatives; and (2) an imperative, which if followed universally, would bring about such antagonism and opposition—illegal imperatives.

Type (*b*) categorical imperatives are unconditional. They must meet two tests: (1) the test of universalizability, by which they are certified as legally correct, and (2) the test of motive. The latter is the requirement that the motive for the fulfillment shall be found in the fact (or belief) that they are *legal*. An imperative like "Do not lie" constrains me to a moral action and is itself apodictic only when it is addressed to my motive to obey it as valid for and obligatory upon others too. An imperative may bind me legally, i.e., may validly restrict my freedom of arbitrary action, regardless of my motive. In this event the imperative is external and belongs to jurisprudence and not to ethics. Other criteria than universalizability may be required to certify them as "practically right," but in the case of negative imperatives such as "*Do not commit perjury*" the criterion of universalizability probably suffices. My motive to obey an imperative like "Write your name in your book" is not expressed in the imperative, as it might be in a hypothetical imperative: "If you want your books returned, write your name in them." But certainly in this case, the *universal* applicability of the imperative is not *my* motive for obedience to it.

It is, I think, safe to say that all categorical imperatives that are in any sense right, and not mere unreasoned and unreasonable commands, are either apodictic or are elliptical assertoric hypothetical imperatives. The categorical imperatives of the second type, therefore, which are of any philosophical interest, are equivalent to imperatives of type (*a*).[37] This is because (*a*) and (*c*) are modally alike, and their formal differences are of little or no philosophical interest.[38]

UNCONDITIONAL (APODICTIC) HYPOTHETICAL
IMPERATIVES

The last type of imperative, (*d*), is the unconditional or apodictic hypothetical, and we must consider it in relation both to the apodictic categorical and to conditional hypothetical imperatives.

An imperative can be both apodictic and hypothetical if its protasis is itself obligation-creating. Obligation-creating protases state problematically that the person to whom the imperative is directed either (*a*) has performed a certain kind of action which creates an obligation, e.g., has made a promise, signed a contract, taken a vow, or the like; or (*b*) is in a certain state or condition which is in part defined by the assumption of special duties and which "contextually implies" specific duties, e.g., is a soldier, a physician, a priest, the only man near the scene of an accident, etc. While the first type of obligation is included under what have been called "*prima facie* obligations" by Ross, I shall refer to the second kind as "*qua*-obligations"; thus, as a soldier, I may have the qua-obligation to do certain actions which I am not obligated to do as a citizen. If the state which creates the qua-obligation is one freely assumed by a moral act, the two types of obligation merge; otherwise they may differ or even conflict. Qua-obligations, like prima facie obligations, may not express what I am *in fact* obligated to do.[39]

The hypothetical imperatives discussed by Kant have as their protases statements of conditions which are not obligation-creating but are statements of natural facts. Mr. Singer, who has recently studied such imperatives in Kant's work, concludes that Kant's failure to distinguish between these two different types of conditions in hypothetical imperatives had the unfortunate effect of causing Kant to shift "from thinking of a categorical imperative as one not conditional upon any purposes of the *agent* to thinking of it as not being conditional upon *anything at all*."[40]

Hence one source of Kant's rigorism, as in the essay on the alleged right to lie.

In this essay I do not propose to examine the question of Kant's rigorism directly, or to discuss further, in Kantian terms, the important distinction between prima facie obligations, qua-obligations, and real obligations. My purpose here is only to point out the manner in which he could have distinguished hypothetical assertoric and problematic imperatives, which he called hypothetical imperatives *simpliciter*, and hypothetical apodictic imperatives, which he did not discuss at all.

In judgments in hypothetical form, we may distinguish between two relations of antecedent and consequent. First, there are judgments in which this relation is real and synthetical: "If there are clouds, it will rain." Second, there are judgments in which the relation is analytic and logical: "If a man is a bachelor, he has no wife." The former can be roughly translated into categorical judgments that are synthetic: "Cloudy days are rainy days," and the latter can be strictly translated into analytic categorical judgments: "Bachelors are unmarried men."

Similarly, there are two types of relation between antecedent and consequent in hypothetical imperatives. The relation is different in "If you want to keep your feet dry, wear your rubbers," and in "If you make a promise, keep it." Unlike hypothetical judgments of both types, which can be translated into categorical judgments, the former imperative cannot be translated into a categorical imperative having the same meaning and scope of relevance. It does not say, "Wear your rubbers," or, if it says this it does so only to those who do not wish to wet their feet.

The hypothetical imperative of the second type becomes, through only verbal change, "Keep your promises." Now while this imperative is not strictly universal, since it contains "your," its address is not as specific as that of the imperative "Wear your rubbers."[41]

If the imperative, "Wear your rubbers" is obeyed, it is not obeyed by anyone because it is a *general* imperative; the reasons why it is obeyed may be stated only in an expanded protasis of the corresponding hypothetical. In this respect, "If you make a promise, keep it" differs from "If you would preserve your good name, keep your promise." The categorical imperative corresponding to the former of these commands is an apodictic imperative under the formula of a categorical imperative; the categorical imperative enunciated in the same sentence (i.e., "Keep your promise") but corresponding to the hypothetical of the first type ("If you would keep your good name...") is not apodictic, does not have the scope of the apodictic, and expresses no necessity.

The hypothetical imperative such as "If you wish to keep your library intact, write your name in your books" has as its antecedent a factual condition, which is related to the consequent only through an empirical causal relation. The declarative sentence reporting obedience to the consequent, i.e., "You do in fact write your name in your books," reports a fact believed to be a causal condition of the end entertained in the antecedent. The fact that a man desires to keep his library intact does not create an obligation to write his name in the book. (He may indeed *say*, "To keep my books from being stolen, I have been obliged to put my name in each volume," but he does not say, "I have had an obligation to put my name in my books." Wants are not the sort of things that create obligations, though to satisfy them we may be "obliged" to do certain other things. "To be obliged to put my name in each book" merely calls attention to the causal necessity or efficacy of an irksome means to a desired end; but "to have an obligation to put the University book plate in each book" calls attention to a qua-obligation of the University Librarian. To be obliged to do something is not, etymology to the contrary notwithstanding, the same as to have an obligation to do it.)

The obedience to the imperative's consequent where the antecedent is obligation-creating is not a means to a state of affairs desiderated or mentioned problematically in the antecedent. The affirming of the consequent by obedience to the imperative is not a means to the accomplishment of the state of affairs envisaged in the antecedent of the hypothetical imperative of the second type; the promise has been made, and we do not say that "fulfilling a promise" is a means to the obedience to the imperative—it *is* the obedience. And certainly fulfilling a promise is not a means to the making of a promise and the obligation to fulfill a promise is not dependent upon whether the fulfilling of the promise is in fact a means to certain purposes entertained in the original making of the promise.

In all these respects, the relation of antecedent to consequent differs in the two types of hypothetical imperative. Mr. Jackson aptly sums up the differences by speaking of the apodosis of hypothetical imperatives of the second type as being "derivatively practically necessary" while the apodosis in those of the first type, which command a means, he calls "derivatively theoretically necessary."[42] Only moral knowledge is required for the practical derivation of apodosis from an obligation-creating protasis, while theoretical knowledge of the world is required for learning what one must do in order to keep his feet dry or to preserve his library.

Given the imperative, "If you want to keep your feet dry, wear rubbers," one may intelligently ask "Why?" and expect an informative answer: "Because the ground is wet, because rubber is impermeable to water.... " But, in Mr. Nowell-Smith's idiom, it is "logically odd" to ask, "Why should I keep my promise?" as a response to "If you make a promise, keep it."[43] The protasis here seems to be a sufficient condition for the apodosis even though it may not *in fact* be sufficient since the apodosis may be *only a prima facie* or *qua*-obligation. But if the question is asked, "I know I made a promise, but why should I keep it?" the question seems to be one that could not be answered by new information on the same level as the fact that a promise has been made;[44] the only appropriate answer to this question would be an exposition of an ethical theory, in which "promise-keeping" would be put under a more general theoretical rubric, etc. Additional reasons to justify this particular apodosis might, in fact, tend to weaken the awareness of the moral connection between promise-making and promise-keeping;[45] and I think this is the principal reason why Kant preferred examples of obligations in which any additional factual information might tend to obscure and impugn the purity of the moral connection between making a promise and keeping it.[46]

I do not say that "You have made a promise" is a sufficient reason for "Keep your promise." Whether I am in fact obligated to keep a promise may depend upon much besides the fact that I have made it, and other facts as well as other obligation-creatings may be relevant to the decision.[47] But that I desire to keep my feet dry is *never* a sufficient reason, and nobody ever believed it was a sufficient reason, for wearing rubbers; and even if I state the sufficient condition, including all relevant facts, the connection between them and the hypothetical imperative. "If you wish to keep your feet dry, wear your rubbers" is not like that in "If you make a promise, keep it."

A full theory of apodictic hypothetical imperatives is not to be found in Kant. But it is not difficult to see what some of its features would be. Such imperatives would be first-order imperatives justified by the formula of what Kant called the categorical imperative, but which we have found to be a formula of an apodictic imperative regardless of its grammatical form. This formula would be a criterion of the admissibility of various kinds of conditions into the protases of the hypothetical imperative that is apodictic. It would tell us what conditions could legitimately and what conditions could not legitimately be included without destroying the apodicticity. The formula would make it possible for us to answer the Kantian question, "Would I be willing for all men to obey the imperative, 'Do A'?" in the form, "Would I be willing for all men under condition C to obey the imperative, 'If C, do A'?" *without trivialization*, since the range of C could be determined by examining the effect of the various possible C's upon the apodicticity of "Do A."[48] It might permit us to show why, for instance, "If you make a promise and find it inconvenient to fulfill it, don't fulfill it," is not an apodictic imperative, while "If you make a promise and find that an innocent person will die if you fulfill it, don't fulfill it" might be an apodictic imperative.

Though a full theory of such imperatives is not developed anywhere in Kant, the *Metaphysics of Morals* is filled with clues as to how it could be done; and such a theory is a desirable addendum to the theory that seems to require moral rigidity and is a desirable foundation for his casuistry. The apparent incompatibility of such hypothetical imperatives with Kant's best known ethical principle vanishes when we realize that "categorical" was not the most suitable adjective for Kant to use in describing the moral imperative.[49]

NOTES

1. *Metaphysics of Morals*, Part 1, *Jurisprudence*, Conclusion (Academy edn., VI, 371).

2. Though Kant explicitly distinguishes "law" from "imperative" and from "rule," he continually uses these words interchangeably, even in §7 of the *Critique of Practical Reason* which professes, in its title, to give as it were the official statement of the "law" but in fact states only an imperative.

3. "Technically practical" and "morally practical" are distinguished in *Critique of Judgment*, Introduction, I.

4. *Foundations*, Academy edn., IV, 414; trans. Beck, p. 31. In *Critique of Practical Reason*, Academy edn., V, 11 (trans. Beck, p. 11), Kant speaks of "problematic, assertoric, and apodictic grounds of determination."

5. *The Categorical Imperative*, p. 115.

6. It seems to have puzzled Kant's contemporaries as much as it puzzles me. See the letter from Schütz to Kant, June 23, 1788 (Academy edn., X, 541). [I subsequently tried to make sense of it in my *Commentary on Kant's Critique of Practical Reason*, pp 144-54. (Added to version reprinted in *Studies*...; see Note 46 below. -hr)]

7. *Metaphysics of Morals*, Part II, *Metaphysical Principles of Virtue*, Introduction, XVIII (Academy edn., VI, 410).

8. See Richard Barber, "Two Logics of Modality [in Kant]," *Tulane Studies in Philosophy*, III (1954), 46.

9. *Metaphysics of Morals,* Part II, *Metaphysical Principles of Virtue,* Introduction, VII (Academy edn., VI, 390).

10. *Critique of Practical Reason,* §1, Remark.

11. *Critique of Pure Reason,* A 75=B 100 n.

12. *Foundations,* Academy edn., IV, 417; trans. Beck, p. 35.

13. There is here no imperative to do *A* unless *A* is known or believed to be a means to *B*. A *purely* problematic protasis could not be the basis for an actual command. Kant in the *First Introduction to the Critique of Judgment* (Academy edn., XX, 200 n.) withdraws the name "problematic imperative" as involving a self-contradiction. But the "mixed problematic imperative," one of whose premises is assertoric, does not involve any self-contradiction in its name. The present analysis shows that each of the hypothetical imperatives of the first type may have a problematic and an assertoric antecedent, and that they differ only in the locus of each modality.

14. *Critique of Practical Reason,* Academy edn., V, 25; *Foundations,* Academy edn., IV, 415.

15. *Foundations,* Academy edn., IV, 417.

16. [In my *Commentary on Kant's Critique of Practical Reason,* pp. 86-87, I modified the position taken here. I there argued that "in what concerns the will" *both* types of imperative are analytical, but in what concerns the understanding, i.e., the content in the choice of means to an end, *neither* is analytical. The meaning of "analytical" as applied to an imperative requires a fuller analysis than I gave it in this paper, but I attempted such an analysis in the *Commentary.* (Added to version reprinted in *Studies...;* see Note 46 below. -hr)]

17. Thus, "Do *A*" corresponds to the indicative, "You ought to do *A*," though the two sentences have different roles in moral discourse. "Do *A*" would not be "practically right" unless "You ought to do *A*" were true.

18. See R. M. Hare, *The Language of Morals* (London: Oxford University Press, 1952), p. 48.

19. By analogy to Broad's terminology in his discussion of the categorical imperative, it might be called "the supreme principle of conditional imperatives." See C. D. Broad, *Five Types of Ethical Theory,* pp. 120-21, 123. I call it a principle of conditional. not of hypothetical imperatives, for we shall see that there are hypothetical imperatives which do not fall under this principle.

20. *Critique of Practical Reason,* Academy edn., V, 34; *Reflection* 6633.

21. *Metaphysics of Morals,* Part II, *Metaphysical Principles of Virtue,* Introduction, VI (Academy edn., VI, 388).

22. *Foundations,* Academy edn., IV, 420 n.; trans. Beck, p. 38 n. The parenthesis in the last sentence of the note indicates that, for a pure or holy will, the imperative would be analytic. Of course it would not be an imperative at all, but only a law; yet in the *Critique* the law is called a priori synthetic. I do not know how to resolve this contradiction. Paton *(The Moral Law* [London: Hutchinson & Co., 1949], p. 142) suggests that "analytic" here has reference to an analytic *argument*.

23. Broad, *Five Types of Ethical Theory,* pp. 120-21, 123.

24. *Critique of Practical Reason,* Academy edn., V, 8 n.

25. *Prolegomena,* §2 c 2.

26. Kant's definitions of analytic and synthetic apply strictly only to subject-predicate propositions, though he uses the terms much more broadly. To identify "analytical" with "logically deducible" would require the application of the term "analytical" to compound propositions containing an argument. Thus: "If (if p then q) and p, then q" might be considered analytical since "If (if p then q) and not q, then p" is self-contradictory. But suffice it to say that Kant does not use the terms "analytic" and "synthetic" to apply to such compound propositions.

27. *Critique of Practical Reason*, §1.

28. *Critique of Pure Reason*, A 159=B 198; *Critique of Practical Reason*, §3, Remark II.

29. *Critique of Practical Reason*, Academy edn., V, 47.

30. *Ibid.*, §7, Remark.

' 31. This is shown in *ibid.*, §§1-7.

32. See especially A 536=B 564.

33. It is interesting to note, in this connection, that in the *Critique of Pure Reason*, in the "Canon," Kant has not developed the concept of autonomy, and therefore does not succeed in connecting morality with the concept of freedom developed in the solution to the third antinomy. At the end of the "Canon," therefore, he treats the concept of freedom as an empirical concept and holds that it is independent of the "transcendental" concept. This is inconsistent with the doctrine of the major ethical works. See M. Gueroult, "Canon de la raison pure et critique de la raison pratique," *Revue internationale de Philosophie*, VIII (1954), 333-57. [I no longer believe that the view in the "Canon" is "inconsistent with the doctrine of the major ethical works"; cf. my *Commentary on Kant's Critique of Practical Reason*, p. 190, n. 40. (Added to version reprinted in *Studies...*; see Note 46 below. -hr)]

34. *Critique of Practical Reason*, Academy edn., V, 47.

35. W. T. Jones, A *History of Western Philosophy* (New York: Harcourt, Brace & World, Inc., 1952), p. 855.

36. This should be clear from the familiar formula of the *Foundations*, but if it is not, the statement in the *Metaphysics of Morals* is unmistakable: "Der kategorische Imperativ, der überhaupt nur aussagt, was Verbindlichkeit sei, ist: Handle nach einer Maxime, welche *zugleich* als ein allgemeines Gesetz gelten kann!—Deine Handlungen mußt du also *zuerst* nach ihrem subjectiven Grundsatze betrachten; ob aber dieser Grundsatz auch objektiv gültig sei, kannst du nur daran erkennen, daß, weil deine Vernunft ihn der Probe unterwirft, durch *denselben* dich *zugleich* als allgemein gesetzgebend zu denken, er sich zu einer solchen allgemeinen Gesetzgebung qualifiziere" (Academy edn., VI, 224; italics added).

37. It is in view of this fact that Kant calls the pragmatic imperative a hypothetical imperative even when the protasis ("Because you want to be happy...") is suppressed. But since "hypothetical" is normally a formal concept, it would be better to call such an imperative "assertoric" when it has no explicit antecedent.

38. They are both called "heteronomous imperatives" by Manfred Moritz, *Studien zum Pflichtbegriff in Kants kritischer Ethik* (Lund: Gleerup Bokförlag 1951), ch. 2, §10.

39. It is incorrect to say, as is often said, that Kant cannot take account of so-called "conflicting obligations." They do not arise in the *Foundations* and the *Critique of Practical Reason*, for there he is concerned only with the formulae for categorical imperatives, and is not concerned with the casuistical problems which arise only on the level of first-order imperatives. He cites them only as examples. In the *Metaphysics of Morals* he

does discuss the concept of "conflicting duties" and denies that the concept is correct, since in any case it is my duty in fact to do only one thing; but he admits the problem of "conflicting grounds of obligation," and this is the problem often erroneously called that of "conflicts of duties." See "Introduction to the Metaphysics of Morals," IV, in Part I of *Metaphysics of Morals* (Academy edn., VI, 224).

40. Marcus G. Singer, "The Categorical Imperative," *Philosophical Review,* LXIII (1954), 581. A similar point is made by A. N. Prior, *Logic and the Basis of Ethics* (Oxford: Oxford University Press, 1949), pp. 40-41. Rashdall had earlier written in the same vein: "Kant...confuses the inclusion of an exception *in* a moral rule with the admission of an exception *to* a moral rule. He does not recognize that the difference between a rule with an exception and a grammatically categorical rule is often purely a verbal one" *(The Theory of Good and Evil* [2 vols.; London: Oxford University Press, 1924], I, 116). Mr. Hare *(Language of Morals,* pp. 50-54) discusses in this connection the difference between "occasional exceptions" and "classes of exceptions." The latter can be specified *in* the rule without affecting its apodicticity, and Mr. Hare says that when so specified the rule is "not looser than it was before, but stricter" (p. 53). (Since this paper was [originally] published, Mr. Singer has elaborated and defended his view in his *Generalization in Ethics* [New York: Alfred A. Knopf, Inc., 1961].)

41. Mr. Hare *(Language of Morals,* pp. 187-90), recognizing that no imperative in ordinary English is strictly universal, proposes an "enriched imperative mood," and in this there would be a universal imperative corresponding to "Keep your promise" but not one corresponding to "Wear your rubbers."

42. Reginald Jackson, "Kant's Distinction between Categorical and Hypothetical Imperatives," *Proceedings of the Aristotelian Society,* 1942-43, 143.

43. Kant would have regarded it as "logically odd." See *Metaphysics of Morals,* Part I, *Jurisprudence,* §19 (Academy edn., VI, 273).

44. New information on the facts would be relevant only in the decision as to whether the prima facie or qua-obligation is really binding.

45. *Foundations,* Academy edn., IV, 394.

46. I have discussed Kant's examples from this point of view in "Sir David Ross on Duty and Purpose in Kant," [*Studies in the Philosophy of Kant* (Indianapolis: Bobbs-Merrill, 1965), pp. 172-73].

47. That such considerations are permitted by Kant, how they are evaluated, and what they are in Kant's work have been exhaustively explored by Paton, "An Alleged Right to Lie. A Problem in Kantian Ethics," *Kant-Studien,* XLV (1954), 190-203; and by Singer, "The Categorical Imperative." See also Mary J. Gregor's *The Laws of Freedom; A Study of Kant's Method of Applying the Categorical Imperative in the Metaphysik der Sitten* (Oxford: Basil Blackwell, 1963).

48. See W. I. Matson, "Kant as a Casuist," *Journal of Philosophy,* LI (1954), 855-60. (Mr. Singer, in his *Generalization in Ethics,* has skillfully spelled out the restrictions expressed in the words *without trivialization;* cf. especially ch. 4.)

49. [This essay originally appeared in *Kant-Studien* 49 (1957), pp. 7-24, and is reprinted with permission.]

The Fact of Reason:

An Essay on Justification in Ethics

INTERNAL AND EXTERNAL QUESTIONS

By the term "external question," which I borrow from Carnap,[1] I refer to a question which concerns the collective justification of all the true propositions contained in any particular realm of discourse. The question of the justification of a judgment within the particular realm of discourse will be called an "internal question."

The problem of justification arises from the belief that no internal question is fully answered until the external question is answered, since the answer to any internal question is hypothetical until the premises are established. The difficulty of the problem arises from the fact that the norms for judging answers to the internal questions are never sufficient for judging answers to the external question.

I shall illustrate the two kinds of questions in logic and in ethics, though the paper as a whole will be concerned only with the question in ethics. An internal question in logic is, for instance, "Why is the syllogism *Baroco* valid?" The answer is given by adducing the *principium de omni et nullo,* which is a principle within logic. But if one asks, "Why is this principle valid?" it seems that no answer can be given. Without this principle, one cannot reason logically at all, and therefore any argument designed to show that it is valid makes use of it on the assumption that it is valid; thus it involves a *petitio principii.* The dictum is the standard for validity of the argument, not the argument a support for the validity of the dictum.

Similarly in ethics. An internal question is, for instance, "Why ought one to tell the truth?" Various answers to this question are given in various ethical theories, but the form of the answer is always the same, viz., by taking recourse to some higher principle within the theory such as, in Kant's theory, the categorical imperative. But one who asked, "Why ought I to tell the truth?" and who is told, "Because the categorical imperative demands it," might then say: "I know that, according to the categorical imperative, I ought to tell the truth; but I want to know why I ought to heed the categorical imperative."

Thus is raised the external question in ethical theory. And it seems to be a question that cannot be answered. An answer would have to be either a factual or a value judgment. If a factual judgment, the answer will not satisfy because we know that no factual statement implies a value judgment. If a value judgment, the original question was not truly an external question, for now the same question can be asked of it.

Kant was aware of the distinction between internal and external questions in ethics. In the *Foundations* the internal question is discussed in the analytical parts, Sections I and II. These Sections give the formula of the moral law and the structure of his ethical system, and thus provide the principles by which every internal ethical question is to be answered. But Kant repeatedly reminds us that nothing in those Sections shows that duty is not "a vain delusion and chimerical notion."[2] To show that duty is a concept with an object, and not merely a concept within a neat logical system, requires the synthetical use of pure practical reason, and a shift from the analytical to the synthetical method of the Third Section. (A similar division, between exposition and deduction, is present, though not so clearly, in the second *Critique*.)

Though Kant's answer to the internal questions of ethics is clear, it is not at all clear what his answer to the external question is. The transcendental deduction of the principle of pure practical reason is, I think, the most obscure part of Kant's ethical theory. It is the purpose of this paper not just to expound what I think Kant's answer to the external question is, but first to explore some possible ways of dealing with the external question and then to examine Kant's method of answering it in the light of its possible alternatives. This preliminary exploration is the more necessary in that the authority of Kant has been invoked by defenders of two dramatically opposite treatments of the problem.

THE INTUITIONISTIC ANSWER TO THE EXTERNAL QUESTION

Taking the external question in its highest generality, "Why ought I to be moral?" the intuitionist answers that one can just see that one ought to be moral, and that is all there is to it. One cannot go farther than that in either logic or ethics: there are clear and distinct self-evident principles of right thinking, and there are clear and distinct self-evident principles of right action, and these are respectively the fundamental principles of logic and of ethics.

While these truths are not, of course, seen with one's physical eyes, the act of apprehending them is more like seeing something than it is like thinking and inferring. To call it "seeing" is to make use of a metaphor, and all the other words which name it likewise seem to be metaphorical also: *Anschauen, intueor,* "apprehend," "grasp," "see by the *lumen naturale*," etc. I shall here use the word "intuition" in two senses, which I shall distinguish as follows. An intuition *in the real sense* is a direct apprehension of an objective truth, value, or state of affairs. An intuition *in the putative sense* is an act which seems to be a real intuition but which in fact may or may not be.

Now it follows from the meaning of intuition in the real sense that if there is an intuition in the real sense of an answer to the external question, ethics is in fact perfectly justified and an otherwise infinite regress of questions and answers is avoided. But I submit that all we have in the way of data are intuitions in the putative sense, that contradictory judgments of intuitions in the putative sense exist, and that there is no valid intuitive means by which real intuitions can be distinguished from putative intuitions.

I do not wish to deny that putative intuitions are common experiences; nor do I wish to deny that some putative intuitions are necessary to provide a kind of

Archimedean platform on which to stand while inquiry is under way. What I do wish to deny is that putative intuitions are self-guaranteeing. For though we would not call a mental act an "intuition" unless we believed that it was in fact revelatory, a putative intuition will seem to be revelatory and will provide an Archimidean platform for inquiry into whether it is in fact a real intuition or not. The necessity that there be an intuition does not guarantee the necessity of any specific putative intuition. To say that in any well-ordered set of propositions for which truth is claimed there is at least one that must be accepted intuitively, if not arbitrarily, is only to acknowledge that not every proposition in the set can be proved. But to say this is not to decide which propositions in the set—or indeed whether any proposition in the set instead of its contradictory—is intuitively certain, where "certainty" is found in a real instead of in a merely putative intuition.

Methodologically, to claim intuitive certainty for any proposition means only:

1) I believe it so strongly that I do not entertain any alternatives.

2) I cannot prove it by deducing it from any proposition about which I have a higher degree of certitude or conviction, so that it seems to be self-guaranteeing as seeing seems to be self-guaranteeing.

3) I must use it in the proof of other propositions which I believe but which I do not claim to be intuitively true.

Each of these conditions is essential, but each is fully met by a proposition which is only putatively intuition. The third of these conditions, however, is fatal to any attempt to claim an intuitive certainty as the answer to an external question, i.e., as the answer to the question of the justification of ethics.

The reason is this. Accepting a given proposition as intuitively true—even calling it a putatively intuitive proposition—requires the prior acceptance of the truth of the other propositions for which intuitive certainty even in the putative sense is not claimed (condition 3). And the real intuitive certainty of the proposition (not just its putative intuitional status) requires the *actual* truth (and not just the belief in the truth) of the propositions which answer internal questions; for if they are false, then by *modus tollens* the putatively intuitive proposition is false and therefore cannot be a really intuitive proposition.

Hence the assertion of the really intuitive truth—assuming we could in fact assert it—is not an additional warrant for the truth of the propositions internal to the system. That is, answering the external question in the manner of the intuitionists—even supposing real intuition to be possible—would not justify the collection of answers to the internal questions, but would rather presuppose some independent warrant for them, and so on ad infinitum.

THE PRAGMATIC ANSWER TO THE EXTERNAL QUESTION

Another procedure in answering the external question is to show that the external and internal questions are so different that the concept of an "answer" is ambiguous. To answer an internal question means to cite a good reason for a yes or no answer. But there is no answer of this shape with a good reason for an external question. Hence the quest for justification is not only in fact futile, but it is misguided from the beginning. It is like asking, "What letter of the alphabet comes before A?" and not being satisfied with the answer, "None," because "none" is not a letter.

Suppose someone asks, "Why should I tell the truth?" and I answer, "Because you ought not to do actions that will probably make you unhappy." The other person may ask me why he should not do this, and I can reply by citing some other more general principle such as "You should respect your own person." For each of my answers, he can respond with another "Why?" Perhaps in exasperation I finally tell him: "At least you will grant that 'You ought to do your duty.' This is an analytical proposition. It would be self-contradictory to say you ought not do your duty. Here, then, is my justification for telling the truth. You granted that each of my answers to your internal questions was correct, but inadequate; and now I have showed you that the first premise of my first prosyllogism is an analytical proposition; therefore the conclusion 'You ought to tell the truth' is logically necessary."

This, however, is not a justification. It would be a justification only if an axiological equivalent of an ontological argument were valid. Kant showed that the concept of a perfect being may analytically imply the concept of an existing being, but that the concept of an existing being does not imply the actual existence of the being. We can show, similarly, that *if* there is anything that one ought to do, it must be his duty to do it; but this hypothetical and analytical judgment does not in the least imply that there is in fact anything that one ought to do. Kant knew this.

Granting this failure to find a validation (*justificatio cognitionis*), an effort is made to find what Feigl[3] has called a vindication (*justificatio actionis*). A vindication is a pragmatic warrant for acting in a certain way (here, giving a set of answers to a set of specific internal questions) without claiming that we know the answers to be cognitively correct, i.e., without claiming that the answers to the internal questions can be known to be true to objective fact or metaphysical essences.

I fear that the belief that validation is impossible may have led the author of this distinction to think that vindication is a substitute for it. But it is not, as I shall try now to show.

To say that an ethical system cannot be validated may mean one of two things. It may mean that we cannot, in principle or in fact, give a justification for it. If Feigl is correct, the principle "*a* is *a*" cannot be justified because we cannot give a justification for it. I shall call such a proposition *participially unjustified*; this term neutrally describes the status of the proposition in question. But to say that a proposition cannot be justified may mean that it is in fact unjustified, i.e., wrong. Again if Feigl is correct, the principle "*a* is not *a*" cannot be justified, but this proposition I shall describe as *pejoratively unjustified*.

Now if we accept the statement, "Ethics as a whole is not validated," then *faut de mieux* we may accept vindication for it, interpreting the sentence to mean that ethics is not participially justified. But there is not the slightest reason why we must interpret the sentence merely participially. Maybe we cannot justify ethics because it is unjustified in the pejorative sense. But—and here is the fatal difficulty—a pejoratively unjustified system may be vindicated just as well as a merely participially unjustified system can be vindicated. Success in use is no guarantee of the rightness of what succeeds, especially when it is a question of the rightness of the test of success itself. If an external validation for an ethical system could be given, it would give that system a unique standing, for if one system is so validated, no rival can be validated. But there is no evidence that only one system can be vindicated; in fact, it is probably false. Vindication is not criterially unique, therefore, and provides no substitute justification for the answer sought along the route of validation.

NEW FORMULATION OF THE EXTERNAL QUESTION

The external question, "Why ought I to be moral?" seems to be logically like the internal question, "Why should I go out in the rain?" But it is not. The internal question admits of two answers: (1) "You should go out, because you have an engagement" or the like; and (2) "You should not." The external question is quite unlike the internal question, inasmuch as it permits at most only one kind of answer, "You ought to embrace this ethical system because...," and its difficulty is due to the fact that we cannot find an answer of this kind, since the because-clause must be a value judgment and the whole answer is then seen as an answer to an internal question. And if one gave an answer of the second kind, viz., "You should not be moral" or "You should reject all ethical systems," this is still a moral judgment, though one that is self-contradictory and hence pejoratively unjustified.

There is another way in which the two questions differ. The internal question asks for information or advice; the external question does not. Suppose someone asks me if it is right for him to do action *X*, and I reply, "No, you ought to do your duty." If he asks why he should, I shall not be able to give him any reasons other than reasons for doing the action *non-X*. That is, the reasons for being moral and for doing one's duty, which he asked for, are not different from the reasons for doing the act which is dutiful, which I have already told him. It is not that there is one set of reasons for being moral, which we do not know, and another set of reasons for doing the moral act, *non-X*, which we may know and have already stated.

Perhaps the terminology of "external and internal questions" has misled us; the questions now seem *toto coelo* different and hardly to fall under the same genus. Let p, q, r, s be a series of internal questions, in which q is a question about the decision of p, r a question about the decision of q, and so on. The so-called external question should not be regarded as the last member of this series, Z, which we approach step-wise. It is not an additional question like the others, but a question about the questions.

Question p has two answers: (a) "You should do it" or (*non-a*) "You should not do it." These possible answers to p constitute the tautology (a or *non-a*), and a tautology materially implies any true proposition. Thus "Either you should go out to keep an engagement, or you should not go out to keep an engagement" entails that the Rhine is a swift river and that Bonn is a lovely city. Among the propositions implied by (a or *non-a*), however, there are some which are necessary for a decision to be made between a and *non-a*.[4] Such propositions I shall call a *presupposition*. Granting a situation of choice, which I shall symbolize as (a or *non-a*), we can ask: What propositions are entailed by the choice of a, and what propositions are entailed by the choice of *non-a*? These propositions constitute answers to the internal question, and if we choose a we are committing ourselves to the system of ethical principles which justify this internal choice; similarly, if we choose *non-a* we are committed to an alternative system of answers to internal questions. But if we ask merely what propositions are entailed by and required for a decision between a and *non-a*, we are asking for the presuppositions which would make a choice between them possible. These presuppositions will be at least part of the answer to the external question, and will constitute the justification for an ethical system about which we shall not be able to ask the same question we could ask about the system of internal answers based on a, or about the system of internal answers based upon *non-a*.

Suppose, for instance, a is the utilitarian decision in some problem of choice, and *non-a* is the answer that would be given by an egoist. A system of propositions entailed by a will be the utilitarian system; the system based on *non-a* might be the egoistic system. About the choice between these systems we might ask the external question, and we have seen how hard it is to answer the question of this kind: after all, why should I consider the interests of others? But the system of propositions entailed by and required for a decision with respect to the choice (a or *non-a*) will not be subject to this kind of question, because it is independent of which of the contradictories we choose. It depends solely upon there being a choice between them.

There are, I think, two possible presuppositions which would provide a decision-procedure for (a or *non-a*). The first is like a throw of a coin: heads I do a, tails I do *non-a*. I know of no way in which anyone could reject this as a valid decision-procedure provided it were *itself* chosen by, say, tossing a coin and not as a result of argument. But immediately the proponent of such a tychistic ethics attempted to argue for it, on whatever grounds, by saying that this was the right way to choose, I think we should have him.[5] For here there would be a choice formally like that between *a* and *non-a*, and he is citing reasons which seem to be valid presuppositions for a choice between deciding to do *a* or, contrariwise, to do *non-a*, so that the question of the justification of either would present insurmountable problems like those we found in the intuitionistic and pragmatistic answers.

What I am suggesting is this: that immediately one gives *any* reason for a choice, there is at work one presupposition which is at least part of the answer to the external question of ethics. This presupposition, I submit, is what Kant called "the sole fact of pure reason." To an examination of this fact I now turn.

THE FACT OF PURE REASON—FIRST INTERPRETATION

Eight times in the *Critique of Practical Reason* Kant uses the expression "fact of pure reason" or "fact of reason." It refers to the ultimate datum of ethics, but what this ultimate datum is, is identified in various ways. The denotata of the term are given as follows:

1) Consciousness of the moral law (Academy edn., V, 31),
2) Consciousness of freedom of the will (p. 42),
3) The law (pp. 31, 47, 91).
4) Autonomy in the principle of morality (p. 42),
5) An inevitable determination of the will by the mere conception of the law (p. 55),
6) The actual case of an action presupposing unconditional causality (p. 104).

In other works there is a similar variety of denotations.[6] Sometimes Kant speaks of the "fact of reason" and sometimes of the "fact of pure reason," and once of the "fact of moral-practical reason." Sometimes he speaks of "fact" *simpliciter,* and sometimes of "fact, as it were."[7]

Because of this variety of terminology, we cannot take Kant's *ipsissima verba* and expect to find a single and unique interpretation for them. At least there seem to be two different kinds of facts referred to.

First, there are the statements that the fact of reason consists in the direct consciousness of something—that is, the fact is the consciousness of the law (1) or of freedom (2). But we have been told elsewhere, and in such a way that leaves no doubt as to Kant's meaning, that we are *not* conscious of freedom, but only of the moral law which is its *ratio cognoscendi*.[8] So let us say that, at least, the consciousness of the moral law is a fact, and that through this fact we become conscious (though not intuitively conscious) of freedom. But we have also been told repeatedly that we do not have indubitable evidence that the concept of duty is valid and that moral ideas are not vain and chimerical.[9] Consequently the indubitable fact that we are conscious of the moral law does not mean that the moral law is itself indubitably valid.

Second, there are statements that what we are conscious *of* is the fact. We are told, in the other passages, that it is a fact of reason that there is a law, that this is a law of autonomy, that this law can determine the will. These are the facts which must be real if morality (at least Kant's conception of it) is to be justified.

This division of meanings of "fact" is perfectly analogous to the division we formulated in the second section, "The Intuitionistic Answer to the External Question," between putative and real intuitions. Consciousness of the law is a putative intuition; and if this consciousness is indeed cognitively veridical, then the law is the object of a real intuition.

Hence Kant's theory of the "fact of pure reason" seems to authorize us to classify him as an intuitionist with respect to the external question; and if my argument in the second section of this essay is correct, we shall have to declare his justification of morality to be inadequate.

THE FACT OF REASON AND THE FACT FOR REASON

In spite of Kant's thinking of the moral law as something directly given to consciousness in the unique experience of respect, I do not think that it is correct to regard him as an intuitionist with respect to the problem of justification. An intuitionist is a kind of Platonist; for him, there is a given Idea or essence, set over against a receptive consciousness which accepts it without mediation or error. But for Kant, the metaphysics of the moral law is not Platonic; the moral law is a creation of reason, and he suggests that it is "merely the self-consciousness of a pure practical reason and thus identical with the positive concept of freedom."[10]

Since I say Kant was not an intuitionist, it is incumbent upon me to find a non-intuitionistic interpretation of the expression "fact of reason." The "of" in this expression may be a subjective or an explicative genitive. Usually it has been interpreted as the former. Heretofore we have interpreted it in the former way to mean a fact known by pure reason as its object, *modo directo* (reason's fact). This is what the fact would be for a genuine intuitionist. But if it is a fact of this kind for Kant, it differs from all other facts (which, for him, must be given in a spatio-temporal intuition), and he would indeed be justified in referring to it as "a fact, as it were."

The "of" in "fact of reason," however, may be an explicative genitive, and will then indicate the fact *that there is pure reason*, a fact known by reason reflexively and not intuitively or *modo directo*. I shall call this "the fact *of* pure reason," while the intuitionistic interpretation of Kant would make us refer only to "the fact *for* pure reason."

If Kant's expressions do mean that he was talking of what I have called the fact *of* reason and not the fact *for* reason, then he is immune to the attack I made upon the intuitionists in the second section. And the fact of reason, as I interpret it, is prima facie independent of the specific moral construction put upon it by

Kant. That is, I am not arguing, for instance, that the fact of pure reason shows that we should not tell a lie. Rather, I am insisting only that there is, in willing, a principle that is rational, whether the willing be moral or immoral, prudent or foolish.[11] If volition appears to be independent of desires and to be morally unconditional, then there must be an unconditionally rational principle for it. The phenomenon of moral obligation implies the fact of reason—the fact that pure reason can be practical—even though in any particular case the judgment of obligation may be wrong. I am not therefore concerned here with the deductive elaboration of Kant's inferences, but with their premises, not with the so to speak metaphysical exposition of the moral principle, but with its transcendental ground.

Only a law which is given by reason itself to reason itself could be known a priori by pure reason and be a fact for pure reason. The moral law, which expresses nothing but the autonomy of reason,[12] can be a fact for pure reason only because it is the expression of the fact of pure reason, i.e., of the fact that pure reason can be practical. That is why the moral law is the sole fact for pure reason; for it expresses only the sole fact of reason. The fact for reason, which we know *modo directo*, is a creation of the fact of reason as legislative. We discover the law not as a given ordinance of God or in an essential structure of a realm of values, for then it would have to be given intuitively. No, we discover the law within volition itself; "If pure reason is actually practical, it will show its reality and that of its concepts in action."[13] It is not a fact (fact *for* reason) which we first discover by a kind of moral intuition and to which we then attempt to conform in our willing.

If this seems to be a slippery argument, let us turn to the moral phenomenon itself. A moral principle is not binding upon a person who is ignorant of it or of the conditions necessary for rational choice according to it. On the other hand, if a person believes that the rational principle is valid for him, then it is in so far forth valid for him. This is true whether the specific principle he follows (e.g., the imperative to do *a*) expresses a claim that is materially valid or not. For only a being aware of the claim of some principle on his choice between *a* and *non-a* could even make a mistake about what he ought to do; if the principle is not acknowledged, there is nothing that he ought (formally) to do. Without a principle there is no possibility of doing right, but also no possibility of doing wrong. To argue against the relevance of some principle is to appeal to normative grounds against the application of normative principles. The rejection of a moral principle is itself a moral act, which can be performed only by a rational being. Hence Kant says: "Every being that cannot act otherwise than under the Idea of freedom is thereby really free in a practical respect."[14] Now "acting under the Idea of freedom" is the same as acting in cognizance of the moral law; hence a person who is conscious of moral constraint (i.e., has a putative intuition of his duty) shows that his reason is practical (even if it is ineffective), i.e., shows the fact *of* pure reason.

If Kant is correct, a pure practical reason can produce only one fact for reason, to wit, the moral law. But I claim only this: even though every specific moral claim that a person acknowledges might be actually invalid (i.e., he might always think that he ought to approve of *a* when, in fact he ought to approve of *non-a*), the adjudication of the conflict between *a* and *non-a* evidences the fact of reason. In this unhappy case, only the derivation of the fact for reason from the fact of reason would be erroneous. But deliberation and responsibility for the choice show that the person will not, in this instance, be able to justify settling the issue between *a* and *non-a* by tossing a coin, but only by appealing to the standard of reason.

To recapitulate: moral consciousness or consciousness of duty is an undisputed fact. Prima facie, it does not justify the assertion that duty is a valid concept, for prima facie it seems to be an intuition of value, *modo directo,* which may be wrong. But the moral law is not only the object of a putative intuition; it is not given to us in the first instance as a fact for consciousness, *modo directo.* The moral law expresses nothing but the law-giving of reason itself, and this legislation is implicit in every rational choice, even though it might happen that every specific law or rule given by an imperfect human reason should in fact be wrong. We might conceivably be wrong in every decision we make, but the decision, if made under the guidance of reason, is a fact or act of reason; and no other act is. (And if Kant is correct, this means that the decision is morally right, for the only fact for reason is the moral law.)

This validity may be called external rather than internal. Internal validity means the rightness of the choice between *a* and *non-a*; external validity means the rightness of choosing between *a* and *non-a* by some rationally chosen standard. To deny this is to make a statement that is pejoratively and not merely participially unjustified.

In this paper, I do not wish to argue, as Kant did, that *Z* which is the presupposition of (*a* or *non-a*) itself implies that *a* is the correct decision or that *non-a* is correct. I do not even wish to argue that there is only one *Z* which is implied by (*a* or *non-a*) and presupposed in its resolution. It is probably true that certain material value principles must be assumed, and that the justification of them would have to be intuitional. My claim is much more modest: it is that *Z*, that reason should govern choice, or that reason is practical, is a presupposition of the act of rational choice between *a* and *non-a*, and a presupposition of the choice of a rational and moral solution of the problem of (*a* or *non-a*). Moreover, it is the presupposition for choice between rational and irrational, between morally responsible and morally irresponsible grounds for deciding on any specific *a*. I am not here proposing the justification of any specific ethical system, such as the Kantian; I am proposing only a Kantian solution for the problem of justification of ethics *überhaupt.*[15]

NOTES

1. Rudolf Carnap, "Empiricism, Semantics, and Ontology," *Revue internationale de philosophie*, IV (1950), 20-40. "We must distinguish," Carnap says, "two kinds of questions of existence: first, questions of the existence of certain entities...*within the framework*; we call them *internal questions*; and second, questions concerning the existence or reality of the *framework* itself, called *external* questions" (pp. 21-22). Although Carnap was concerned with existence only of such "entities" as numbers, things, properties, classes, and propositions, his distinction can easily be applied to "entities" like values and duties. Carnap tries to show that external questions have no epistemological meaning and are thus pseudo-questions. Such external questions show only that we arbitrarily assume or reject "the forms of expression for the framework in question." Opposed to this is the thesis of this essay: if the framework is itself a value-system (system of value judgments, imperatives, or obligations), answers to internal questions leave no elbowroom for arbitrary answers to the external question. The form of the internal answer determines the abstract form of the external answer; the internal question itself implies a distinct kind of answer to the external question. In this respect, theoretical and practical questions are different. If Carnap is correct in the problem of theoretical questions, one cannot infer from that that his theory can be simply applied to practical questions. I do not here raise the question of whether his solution to the theoretical question is correct.

The conclusions reached in this paper have a marked resemblance to those of C. I. Lewis in his *The Ground and Nature of the Right* (New York: Columbia University Press, 1955), though the form of the argument is very different. I owe important suggestions concerning the concept of "presupposition" to Dr. Patricia A. Crawford; see her "Kant's Theory of Philosophical Proof," *Kant-Studien*, LIII (1962), 257-68. I wish to thank Professor Johannes-Erich Heyde of Berlin for a terminological suggestion, which I have followed, in the analysis of the expression "fact of reason."

2. *Foundations*, Academy edn., IV, 402; trans. Beck, p. 18.

3. Herbert Feigl, "Validation and Vindication," in *Readings in Ethical Theory*, ed. Wilfrid Sellars and John Hospers (New York: Appleton-Century-Crofts, Inc., 1952), pp. 667-80; "De principiis non est disputandum...?" in M. Black, *Philosophical Analysis* (New York: Prentice-Hall, Inc., 1963).

4. This will be modified in the second paragraph following this.

5. See C. I. Lewis, *The Ground and Nature of the Right*, p. 86.

6. The fact is: (*a*) freedom (*Critique of Judgment*, §91 [Academy edn. V, 468]);

(*b*) the law of freedom (*Metaphysics of Morals*, Part I, *Jurisprudence*, §6 [Academy edn., VI, 252]);

(*c*) that the law is in us *(Vorarbeiten zur Tugendlehre*, Academy edn., XXIII, 378);

(*d*) the categorical imperative (*Opus postumum*, Academy edn., XXI, 21).

(*a*) corresponds most closely to (5) and (6); (*b*) to (3) and (4); (*c*) and (*d*) to (1).

7. The many variations in his terminology are explored in my *Commentary on Kant's Critique of Practical Reason*, ch. 10, §2, especially p. 166 nn.

8. *Critique of Practical Reason*, Academy edn., V, 4 n.

9. *Foundations*, Academy edn., IV, 402.

10. *Critique of Practical Reason*, Academy edn., V, 29; trans. Beck, p. 29.

11. See my *Commentary on Kant's Critique of Practical Reason*, pp. 84, 109.

12. *Critique of Practical Reason*, Academy edn., V, 33.

13. *Ibid.*, p. 3; trans. Beck, p. 3.

14. *Foundations,* Academy edn., IV, 448 n.; trans. Beck, p. 66 n.

15. [This essay originally appeared in *Kant-Studien* 52 (1960), pp. 271-82, and is reprinted with permission.]

Kant's Two Conceptions of the Will
in their Political Context

In the *Critique of Practical Reason*, the concept of will is ambiguous. Theories of the freedom of the will which seem to have no connection with each other are presented side by side. The reader does not readily see that they are compatible with each other, for Kant does not make it clear that there are two conceptions of the will and that the concept of freedom applied properly to the one is different from the concept of liberty applied to the other. If one does not carefully distinguish the two conceptions, not only the Kantian moral philosophy but also his political theory appears to run into an impasse. If, in order to avoid this impasse, we establish not only a distinction between the two conceptions but go to the other extreme and think that the two conceptions apply to distinctly different and opposed faculties, one of several ethical and political doctrines will be presented as uniquely and genuinely Kantian, and the others will be discarded. The object of this brief essay is to make the necessary distinctions, and then to establish the connections between them so as to modify three one-sided and extreme views of Kant's social and political teaching.

I

The *Critique of Practical Reason* inherits, from the two preceding works, two different conceptions of the will, but it does not indicate clearly the difference between the two.[1] Only in reading the *Metaphysics of Morals* does one see Kant, with an appropriate terminology, distinguish between them. The principal writings of Kant had been written without this clarification, and it is somewhat difficult to go back and apply the later distinction in the earlier works in every place where it is necessary for full clarity. It can and ought to be done, though some difficulties will still remain, since the explicit definition of the two concepts in the *Metaphysics of Morals* itself is not without ambiguity.

From the *Critique of Pure Reason* there comes the concept of freedom as spontaneity, the faculty of initiating a new causal series in time. The first *Critique* does not profess to demonstrate that this is a "real concept," i.e., a concept that really has an object. It shows simply that there is nothing logically impossible in it, and that though it is not necessary to the study of nature by theoretical reason, it is necessary if the structure of theoretical reason is to be perfected. It is nonetheless true that Kant, in 1781, believed that it was a concept applicable to the human will and that it applied to spontaneous and voluntary actions, though the same actions were comprehended, theoretically and empirically, under the causal laws of nature. In the first *Critique* (except for the "Methodology"), Kant was little occupied with problems of moral philosophy. Still, he knew already that a good will is a free will which obeys a moral law, though the formula and the source of this law were not developed in the *Critique of Pure Reason.*

The search for the formula and source of the law for a spontaneous will constitutes the principal task of the *Foundations of the Metaphysics of Morals*. In this little book, however, there appears an entirely new concept of freedom, viz., that of autonomy. Autonomy refers to the creator of law. An autonomous or free will is a will subject to no law except one of which it is itself the author; it is a will independent of any law (like the laws of nature) which has any other source. The faculty which, in this sense, is strictly autonomous is "pure practical reason," and Kant identifies it also with will.

Thus appears the ambiguity of which I have spoken. Kant speaks generally of the spontaneous initiation of a causal series as emerging in an act of will; and he speaks of the source of the law to which this spontaneity is subject as also a will. But the two conceptions are obviously different, and much later Kant tried to establish the difference between them by introducing a terminological distinction between *Willkür*[2] and *Wille*.[3]

Kant had often previously used these words, sometimes to intimate a tacit distinction which he had not fully developed in his own thought; but more often the words seemed to be interchangeable. And, further, even after he had established the distinction, Kant often did not remain faithful to it; it has been wittily said of Kant that he succeeded in being technical without being precise. Yet I do not believe that he ever used the word *Willkür* when he meant to say *Wille* in a strict sense (though the converse error is common).

The formal definition of *Wille* given in the *Critique of Practical Reason* is: "A power to determine the causation [of an act] by the representation of rules."[4] This is the concept already made familiar in the first *Critique*. Since reason is required[5] to derive an act from a rule, law, or maxim, one can say that the will is nothing but practical reason; it is this faculty which makes a rule of reason the efficient cause of an action by means of which an object can be realized, or the means by which one goes from mere idea to the state of affairs envisaged in it. *Wille* is distinguished from simple desire since it is never determined by the object or even by our concept of the object, but always by a law which can be formulated only by reason, although its application may be to the endeavor for objects of desire.[6] If the motive for an action is found in the lower faculty of desire, it is solely a conception of the object and is always empirical, whether the conception be clear and rational or sensible and confused. The higher faculty of desire is will, which always operates (and not just when it is morally good will) according to a rule presented exclusively by reason (which can be either pure or empirical reason). An impulse and a conception of an object being given as a condition of action, the use of reason, in this case, is solely for the purpose of choosing specific rules for achieving the goal of desire. Reason, in this sense, is the art of inference, more specifically here, the art of practical inference. It is here a question of the *usus logicus* of practical reason; it is comparable to general logic which, as not concerned with the content of knowledge but only with its form, is the *usus logicus* of theoretical reason (i.e., the art of syllogism).[7]

The faculty thus defined and here named *Wille* is, much later, identified by Kant with *Willkür*. It is the faculty of choosing an object which is left incompletely determined by the rule or maxim given, in universal form, by reason. *Willkür*, therefore, is not exclusively pragmatic in its action; it can be moral. Whether it is pragmatic or moral depends upon the condition[8] of the rule it follows. In each act of volition, there is a material,[9] some object of desire; but it is not necessary to select the rule with respect to our knowledge of the causal conditions under which the object can be realized. If that is a condition for the choice of the rule, the rule is pragmatic or technical. If, on the other hand, it is a rule which specifies the form which every specific technical rule must take, that is, a rule that the maxim of the action ought itself to be universally applicable to rational beings, then the rule is a moral rule. The *logical* use of reason is the same in the moral and in the pragmatic action. But in moral action, there is another use of reason. It is the *usus realis* of reason, and it is this use which defines the function of pure practical reason.

By contrast with *Willkür*, we have thus a concept of will not as directly determining an action by a rule applied for the satisfaction of an impulse, but a concept of will insofar as it is the legislator of maxims of which we are conscious in the voluntary actions of *Willkür*.

The rule of reason still leaves undetermined the choice of the object of *Willkür*, but we are now concerned not with this determination but with the origin of the rule of reason itself. If this rule of reason is derived from our empirical or theoretical knowledge of the causal conditions for achieving an object of desire, there is nothing new in the problem; theoretical or cognitive reason furnishes the knowledge that "*A* causes *B*," and practical interest in *B* converts this into "*A* is a means of attaining *B*."

In moral action, the rule cannot have such a material content as its condition, for it would not then be universally valid but valid only on the condition that *B* was desired. The source of the rule, therefore, cannot be theoretical reason, and the origin of the rule cannot be attributed to the *usus logicus* of reason, even to the *usus logicus* of practical reason. Thus reason must have a real use: it should be seen as the faculty of formulating a priori synthetic rules. This corresponds to the use that reason has in transcendental logic (with regard to the formation of theoretical a priori synthetic judgments), and not to the use of reason in general logic, which is solely concerned with the form and implications of the form of judgments. After the *Critique of Pure Reason,* this use of reason is familiar to us in its theoretical function. The second *Critique*, in establishing that there is a *pure* practical reason, establishes in the same way the fact that practical reason has a *usus realis* and not merely a *usus logicus*.

The difference between the pure reason of the first and the pure reason of the second *Critique* is not found in the difference between *usus realis* and *usus logicus*, but in the kind of a priori synthetic judgments established by reason. If the judgment is practical, that is to say, if it is a rule for *Willkür*, reason is practical, and pure practical reason is then identified with the moral will.

It thus appears that we now have two concepts of will, totally different from each other. The one, which is called *Willkür* in the *Metaphysics of Morals*, we may refer to as an executive faculty. The other, which is pure practical reason, is *Wille* in the strict sense, and may be called a legislative faculty. "From *Wille* there arise laws; from *Willkür,* maxims."[10] *Willkür* is obliged to execute that which pure practical reason in its real use (not its logical use) makes law. Thus, in the final analysis, there are not two distinct wills or two different faculties related only in an external or coercive manner. We find *Wille* and its laws by means of a regression upon the conditions of *Willkür*, not by separating them and turning towards some external legislator (God or nature) for *Willkür*. We are immediately conscious of the moral law every time we conceive of a maxim for our will (though here Kant says, incorrectly, *Wille* when he means *Willkür*).[11] *Willkür*, the faculty of spontaneity, is wholly spontaneous only when its action is governed by a law of pure practical reason, not when it accepts a rule given by nature for the accomplishment of some desire. Pure reason is effective, that is practical, only upon the acceptance of its law as a motive (*Triebfeder*) by *Willkür*. Its law is never a law of action, but a law for the choice of maxims for an action; it leaves specific action undetermined, and *Willkür*—desire, plus the logical use of reason, plus consciousness of the maxim which expresses the condition of the rule—determines the action itself.

We must now consider the word "freedom" since it is attributed to will in each of the conceptions. *Willkür* is free to the extent that the conception of any law of reason controls its actions, and the degree to which it is in fact free at any moment is an empirical question. We discover (empirically) that man has an *arbitrium liberum*, not an *arbitrium brutum*.[12] This is the freedom which Kant calls "comparative." In this comparative sense, freedom is not a question of the will as such, but of a simple desire subjected to some degree of rational control. Thus the *arbitrium liberum* can in fact be only a part of the mechanism of nature.[13] To show that it is morally free, it is necessary not to question its power to occasion changes in the world, but to inquire into the provenance of the law which is included in its maxims. If the latter comes from the apprehension of nature, then comparative freedom is not moral freedom. *Willkür* is morally free in the measure that its maxims are chosen because they conform to the law of pure practical reason, i.e., to the law that the maxims of a rational being are to be universally valid and that the actions of a moral being ought to be based on maxims chosen because they are valid for all rational beings. Though all its actions unfold in the order of nature, and though they can, in principle, be predicted by virtue of our knowledge of the laws of nature, they are nonetheless free actions and we are responsible for them, since they are chosen with respect for a law which is not determined by the state of affairs in nature.

This is the liberty of *Willkür*. But what is the freedom of pure practical reason of *Wille* in the narrow sense? It is not free in the sense of being indeterminate, of being free of fetters or in possessing a supernatural spontaneity. It does not possess freedom, Kant once tells us, because it does not act at all.[14] Its freedom is its purity, the nonempirical character of the universal law which it gives. It is freedom in the sense of autonomy. Autonomy is the faculty of making laws by itself and for itself, and the term autonomy applies not only to pure practical reason, but to pure reason in general.

We can now summarize and bring the two concepts together. *Willkür* is *completely* free, i.e., spontaneous, only when it adopts as its law an autonomous decree of pure practical reason or *Wille*. By a kind of hybridization of concepts, we speak of an autonomous *Willkür* and a spontaneous *Wille*. Still, it is better to speak of a free and spontaneous *Willkür* which is not naturally determined as being free in what Kant calls the negative sense, and of an autonomous *Wille* as being free in what Kant calls the positive sense of freedom.[15]

II

One of the principal difficulties in moral philosophy before Kant was this: if freedom of choice is granted, how can one subject it to the law and make it moral? The history of the philosophy of the eighteenth century is full of attempts to respond to this question. The most typical one was that there was a motive of the will which was different from the knowledge of the law, and which was added to this knowledge, such as the desire for happiness, or the desire for recompense for certain actions, or the love of God. Since Kant saw clearly that there was a generic difference between morality and prudence, between a truly good will and a will prudent in following its own interests, this kind of answer did not suit him. All explanations of this kind are heteronomous, i.e., are dependent upon conditions which have to be discovered empirically and which are destructive of the universal necessity which is the mark of moral obligation. For morality, the consequences of such a heteronomous empiricism are comparable to those of strict empiricism in our knowledge of nature. Both, Kant believed, led to skepticism.

The response Kant made to this question is his most important contribution to moral philosophy. That the will of man both creates and executes obligations is one of the most dramatic theses in Kant's philosophy. It is as dramatic as, and comparable to, the "Copernican Revolution" of his theoretical philosophy. As long as the origin of the law, be it natural or be it moral law, was ascribed to the nature of things and as long as it was believed that it could be known only by means of experience, its universality and necessity were illusory. Although one might well be a theoretical skeptic in the manner of Hume, for Kant skepticism in matters of morality seemed to be at once unfounded and ungenuine, and immoral in its effects.

It was known to some of Kant's predecessors that the moral law is rational and is discovered a priori and that it is an obligation of man to render obedience to this law without regard to the reward which followed—at least one believed it followed—the obedience. That morality is the pursuit of a perfection, and that the realization of a perfection is accompanied by pleasure, was recognized by

Wolff, for example, who did not fall into the common error of thinking that it was the accompanying pleasure rather than the perfection itself which was the object of choice. But no one seemed to know why one should choose perfections nor how to determine what they were and how to approach them. Their error, Kant thought, was that of trying to establish practical conduct on tautologies. To avoid the tautologies, the disciples of Wolff (e.g., Baumgarten) surreptitiously reintroduced all the hedonistic and eudaemonistic elements which Wolff had, at least officially, suppressed. Kant admitted that that was the only thing they could do; all their material principles, however rationalistically conceived, were only principles of self-love and private happiness.

Now because Kant discovered the law as a product of pure reason and as rendered evident by "the sole fact of pure reason," and because he did not have to try to obtain it from the abstract concept of perfection or the concept of Wolff's "will in general," it was possible for him to see that the will as "creator of the law" was an idealization of the spontaneous *Willkür*. Granted that, Kant did not have to look for exterior motivation for obedience to that law, nor support it by any appeal to the authority of God or nature. Rational personality as initiator of the laws is a being which is *ipso facto* an ought for partially rational beings. Or, put another way, the duty of which we are conscious as constraining the actions of our *Willkür* is a product of law on impulse; the law would be a law which *Willkür* would obey spontaneously if *Willkür* did not have an impulsive element and did not to some extent lack rationality. The same faculty, as a pure faculty, initiates the laws and, as sensibly affected, is bound to obey them. "One need only analyze the sentence which men pass upon the lawfulness of the actions to see in every case that their reason, incorruptible and self-constrained, in every action holds up the maxim of the will [*Willens*] to the pure will [*Willen*], i.e., *to itself regarded as a priori practical.*"[16]

Thus Kant can say that the law and the conditions necessary to obedience to it—the spontaneity of *Willkür*—have one common source, a source which his predecessors did not discover and of which they hardly even felt the need. His predecessors, therefore, were never able to translate their formalistic ontological ethic into a practical doctrine without destroying either the formality of their ontological principle or the purity of the conception of the moral law. All too often, in their ignorance, they did both.

The central point of the Kantian philosophy was anticipated only by Rousseau. It is so essential in the philosophy of Kant that I propose to call it, by analogy to the "Copernican Revolution," the "Rousseauistic Revolution" in moral philosophy. Rousseau said simply: We are not obligated to obey any law in whose establishment we have not participated. Obligation to any other law is slavery, and obedience to it can be obtained only by a system of reward and punishment in which there is no place for dignity; but obedience to a law one gives oneself is freedom. Others saw in law only a restriction on freedom, a restriction no doubt necessary, but all the same a restriction. Rousseau said: Valid law is an expression of freedom. Kant suggests: "Moral law is nothing else than the self-consciousness of pure practical reason, and is thus equivalent to freedom."[17]

While Rousseau established the essential connection between law and freedom primarily in the political sphere, where his doctrine was adopted with little change by Kant, the doctrine of autonomous government by free citizens of a republic is deepened by Kant into a moral, metaphysical, and even religious conception. Precisely because he developed this doctrine in his theoretical ethics more than Rousseau did, we are in a better position to clarify his political doctrines than we are to clarify those of Rousseau. We can easily see how diverse political views, often imputed to Rousseau and even occasionally to Kant, can be explained, or reconciled, or refuted by turning to the fundamental differences in the two conceptions of will in the principal ethical writings of Kant.

For though it is not hard to find in reading Rousseau an ideology for anarchy or for fascism, it is not so easy to consider Kant under either aspect (though some efforts have been made in these directions). The reply to such efforts is to recall the specific senses of freedom or liberty as related to his two conceptions of will.

III

The specific question is: Can the human will be, at once, spontaneous, obedient, and autonomous? These prima facie incompatible attributes can belong to it, if Kant is right. They must belong to it if he is correct, since each involves the others. But if spontaneity and obedience to law are taken in superficial forms, or if obedience and liberty as political concepts are taken in a superficial form, paradoxes can be found in Kant's ethical theory and in his social and political teachings that are exactly parallel to those which have been found, perhaps with more warrant, in Rousseau's. There are three.

1) Kant is individualistic in his ethics and in his political doctrines. But the moral person is only an abstraction for him, a bearer of a formal potential good will, which is supposed to dominate the concrete individual person who, in his specific characteristics, is the locus of moral and political freedom. Hence Kant's individualism is empty; all right and obligation are universal, and all individuals are conceived as so abstractly equal not only in rights but also in obligations that no social system could be made with them.

2) Kant is universalistic in his ethics and in his political doctrines. But the universalism is formal and empty; for the locus of freedom and responsibility lies in the legislation of the individual, and the social and universalistic aspect of morality is left ungrounded, since the latter is necessarily an outward restriction on inward spontaneity and individual freedom.

3) Kant is libertarian and individualistic in his ethical theory, but in order to give form and substance to the social and political dimension of morality, he provides a doctrine of obedience at all costs that is the political opposite of free-

dom and individualism. The "liberty" he espouses is in actuality that of an army or totalitarian state, not of individuals.

Quite apart from the fact that the objections to Kant expressed in the first two points are incompatible with each other, and that the one cancels the other out—the third being a kind of synthesis of the first two—it is possible to show that none of them is valid. Each arises from a misinterpretation of the conception of will, and associated with this are errors of interpretation of the concepts of autonomy, obedience, and spontaneity.

Each of these criticisms, if fully expanded, would entail the supposition that in Kant's doctrines there are two wills, externally related and necessarily opposed to each other, so that the perfection of one is the ruin of the other. Which paradox is drawn depends upon the critic's belief concerning which of the conceptions is the more important to Kant (which happens, of course, to be the one less important to the critic; for such are the ways of philosophical dialectic).

If the *Wille* or pure practical reason as an abstract, epistemic or moral concept is so emphasized that it is made to do the job of execution as well as legislation, being interpreted as fully determining the action to be undertaken, the individual *Willkür* is restricted and is not free. Thus we have the first paradox. This is perhaps the most common of all criticisms of Kant, and is the basis of the charge that there is in his philosophy no place for casuistry and hence no legitimation for a realistic political theory. Recent studies of the casuistic elements in Kant's ethical writings suffice to show that this criticism is not well founded historically.[18]

If, on the other hand, the maxim is thought of as issuing from the individual's private and unique *Willkür*, it is not possible to see how the maxims decreed will meet the requirements of social uniformity and harmony or how, indeed, they could make any claim to be binding upon others.[19] Hence arises the second paradox, which the romanticists exploited, in their use of Kant in their moral and political theory—to whom Kant replied in advance in his *What is Orientation in Thinking?*

Finally, if the *Wille* is given an institutionalized form and expression, say in the state, and the *Willkür* is left with power but no authority, it is something to be thwarted and tamed or eradicated, and there results the tyranny of "Prussianism."[20] This is thought to be a realistic, political application of the third of the paradoxes, which separates the individual-moral from the social-political elements of the first two.

But the answer to all of them is that there are not two wills. There is one will, with its formal universal condition which is universally valid practical reason, and with its material condition which depends upon the specific involvement of the individual in the peculiar circumstances of his world at his time and place. Without the former, there is no law; without the latter, there is no deed. The former is the Kantian equivalent of Rousseau's *volonté générale*; the latter is the ingredient in the *volonté des tous* of Rousseau. But whereas Rousseau taught that the former could be determined in fact only by a vote of the latter,

Kant thought it could be approached through a regression upon the conditions of the latter, upon the conditions which give to the latter whatever degree of freedom and spontaneity it can possess.

The alleged paradoxes are not so much paradoxes of an inherent dualism in Kant's ethics as they are manifestations of a paradoxical predicament of human life itself. We find in ourselves individualized manifestations of universal mandates and injunctions. Man is the only being in the world that can get himself entangled in these paradoxes, with all the horror they bring and all the heroism they demand. For man is the only being in the world who is a citizen of two worlds, and subject to both psychological explanation and moral exhortation; he is the only being in the world who is torn between the roles of spectator and actor. He alone can issue, recognize, obey, disobey (and not merely illustrate or fail to illustrate) laws. If he were a beast, he could neither create nor obey laws; were he a god, he could create them without having to obey; were he a slave, he would have to obey but could not create laws. But he is, for good or evil, neither beast nor slave nor God.[21]

Had the Kantian teaching avoided either of the first two paradoxes by really separating the will into two faculties, it would have been less responsive and faithful to the fatefully paradoxical aspect of human life itself, for it would have edged man a little nearer to being a slave (paradoxes 1 and 3) or a god (paradox 2).

The greatest error possible in the interpretation of Kant—an error so great that it must seem to be politically or ideologically motivated—is that which leads to the third of the paradoxes. According to this, Kant esteemed obedience so highly that neither moral nor political freedom could exist as more than polite names for obedience to tyranny; and such a doctrine does not stop, any more than the historical impulse it represents, with making men slaves; it regards them as beasts in the mechanism of nature, which may of course include the arbitrary edicts and powers of tyrants.

Fortunately, this greatest error is the one easiest to refute. This error not only separates one will into two, but locates each in a different person (or institution), each of which is in conflict with the other. The end result is that rights are ascribed to one, and only the duty to obey is ascribed to the other. But if the Kantian answer to the first two criticisms is subtle and must be ferreted out, that to the third is clear and forceful in Kant's own words, and does not require a reconstruction or reinterpretation of the texts in the light of the distinction between two meanings of the concept of will and freedom. For Kant says:

> With regard to the most sublime reason in the world that I can think of with the exception of God—say, the great Aeon—when I do my duty in my post as he does in his, there is no reason under the law of equality why obedience to duty should fall only to me and the right to command only to him.[22]

Accordingly, Kant quotes with approval (but with a certain arch cynicism, too) the apothegm of Frederick the Great that he was the servant of his people.[23] This pretended separation of rights from duties, of obligation-creation from obligation-execution, ignores the fact that all moral discipline is self-discipline, from which it follows that all just government is self-government. The same man, by virtue of the same faculty in its legislative and executive functions, its formal and its material conditions, is at the same time the subject and the sovereign both in the realm of ends and in the just political state. Kant's doctrine of man in the state, therefore, does not hold that he can be or ever should become merely an abstract citizen, participating abstractly and uniformly in a *volonté générale;* nor does it hold that he is and must necessarily remain an animal to be tamed only by police machinery working for an alien law. With Rousseau, Kant finds man the citizen as the a priori condition of man as exercising all his spontaneous capacities against the merely natural, i.e., the nonpolitical and the nonmoral, mechanism of life.

That this is the proper Kantian order of political and moral concepts is shown clearly in his essays on the philosophy of history and in his conception of the moral commonwealth (the Church invisible) in his book on religion. In each case, the first step of mankind from barbarism to morality is the step into civil society, in which man the animal is tamed into man the citizen, in a state in which virtue can be slowly developed out of its social and political counterfeits. Only along this path does the free *Willkür* develop out of the *arbitrium brutum,* and finally the maxim of pure practical reason become the determinant of action.[24]

NOTES

1. This was pointed out, and its importance emphasized, by Victor Delbos, *La philosophie pratique de Kant* (2nd edn.; Paris: Alcan, 1926), p. 455.

2. On the difficulties of translating these words, see my *Commentary on Kant's Critique of Practical Reason,* p. 177 n. (I wish now to call attention to the review of this book by John R. Silber in *Ethics,* LXXIII (1963), 179-97, the second part of which is a scholarly study of *Wille* and *Willkür.*)

3. "The faculty of desire which operates under concepts, in so far as the principle which determines it to action is in itself and not drawn from objects, is called the faculty of arbitrarily doing or refraining. As related to the consciousness of the power to act to produce the object, it is called *Willkür....* The faculty of desire of which the internal principle of determination resides in the reason of the subject is called *Wille....* [The latter] is practical reason itself" *(Metaphysics of Morals,* Academy edn., VI, 213).

4. *Critique of Practical Reason,* Academy edn., V, 32; trans. Beck, p. 32.

5. *Foundations,* Academy edn., IV, 412.

6. *Critique of Practical Reason,* Academy edn., V, 60.

7. *Inaugural Dissertation,* §§5, 6.

8. On this use of the word "condition," see my *Commentary on Kant's Critique of Practical Reason,* p. 81.

9. *Critique of Practical Reason,* Academy edn., V, 34.

10. *Metaphysics of Morals*, Academy edn., VI, 226.

11. *Critique of Practical Reason*, Academy edn., V, 29.

12. *Critique of Pure Reason,* A 534=B 562.

13. *Ibid.*, A 803=B 831.

14. *Metaphysics of Morals,* Academy edn., V1, 226.

15. *Critique of Practical Reason,* Academy edn., V, 33; *Metaphysics of Morals,* Academy edn., V1, 213-14.

16. *Critique of Practical Reason,* Academy edn., V, 32; trans. Beck, p. 32. It would have been preferable to have said *Willkür* for *Wille* and *Wille* for pure will. Italics added.

17. *Critique of Practical Reason,* Academy edn., V, 29; trans. Beck, p. 29.

18. See, for example, W. 1. Matson, "Kant as Casuist," *Journal of Philosophy*, LI (1954), 855-60; H. J. Paton, "Kant on Friendship," *Proceedings of the British Academy*, XLII (1956), 45-66; Fr. Marty, "La typique du jugement pratique pur, la morale kantienne et son application aux cas particuliers," *Archives de philosophie*, 1935, No. 1, pp. 56-87; and my "Apodictic Imperatives," [pp. 28-44 above]. I would now add Mary Gregor's book, *The Laws of Freedom* [(Oxford: Basil Blackwell, 1963)].

19. This is the criticism in George Santayana's intemperate book, *Egotism in German Philosophy* (New York: Charles Scribner's Sons, 1916), pp. 50-51 in the second edition (1940).

20. This criticism is stated, but not wholly endorsed, by John Dewey, *German Philosophy and Politics* (1895), p. 122. But Dewey did argue that "Prussianism" could arise from Kantianism because "the two worlds of Kant were too far away from each other" and could be connected only through the idealistic theory of history and the state—a theory with definitely totalitarian political consequences.

21. *Metaphysics of Morals*, Academy edn., VI, 241.

22. *Perpetual Peace*, Academy edn., VlIl, 350 n.; trans. L. W. Beck, "Library of Liberal Arts," No. 54 (New York: Liberal Arts Press, 1957), pp. 11-12 n. God only is excepted because he is under no law (in the form of an imperative). That is, as a holy will there is no obligation for God. But the same moral law is perfectly manifested in His holiness and imperfectly manifested in our virtue.

23. *Ibid.*, p. 352; trans. Beck, p. 14.

24. [This essay originally appeared in *Annales de philosophie politique* 4 (1962), pp. 119-37.]

Once More unto the Breach:

Kant's Answer to Hume, Again

It is a continuing scandal of philosophical scholarship that after nearly two centuries the question must still be debated: *What* was Kant's answer to Hume? Until there is agreement about this, there is little reason to hope that the philosophical problem of the adequacy of a theory like Kant's to answer questions raised by a theory like Hume's can be solved.

Two recent contributions[1] ascribe to Kant much the same answer. Mrs. Schipper (p. 73) holds that the existence of objectively valid physical science is a fundamental hypothesis of Kant and that this science presupposes the law of causality; hence, she concludes by a magnificent *non sequitur*, "We can have knowledge of such a necessary sequence, since we presuppose it in our laws or 'legislate it to nature'" (p. 74). One is reminded of Lord Russell's acute remark that presupposing has all the advantages over demonstrating that theft has over honest labor.

The second author criticizes Mrs. Schipper's paper for giving neither "an answer to Hume's problem nor...Kant's definitive solution" (p. 71); but seven pages later she concludes that "Kant has shown that the human mind, *if it is to have certain knowledge,* must employ the categories as the a priori presuppositions of Experience" (pp. 77-78, italics added). Of course if we are to say we have certain knowledge, then we must reject the arguments or premises of the skeptic who has striven to show that we do not. There is nothing in the logic of these two papers that Kant would have embraced more gladly than he would have espoused those "who took for granted that which [Hume] doubted, and demonstrated with zeal and often with impudence that which he never thought of doubting."[2]

Professor Wolff's recent book has dealt with the problem of Kant's answer to Hume at great length and with admirable subtlety.[3] Inasmuch as Professor Wolff has paid me the compliment of taking one of my footnotes very seriously and has written an extended criticism of the argument it contained in concentrated, indeed inspissated, form, I should like to comment upon his argument and, at more length and with thanks to his careful analysis, try to make my argument somewhat stronger. Wolff summarizes my argument in the following words:

> A regressive analysis beginning from mathematics and science will not refute Hume, for mathematics and science is [*sic*] precisely what Hume professes to doubt. But if the very same principles (premises) which produce (imply) science and mathematics also imply the distinction between even apparently objective and subjective, etc., etc., then Hume will have been convincingly answered, for not even he can deny them.[4]

Now Wolff's criticism of me is like mine of Schipper and Williams: the regressive method does not prove the truth of the premises even if the truth of the conclusion is assumed. Such an argument merely affirms a consequent. Since I was fully alert to the danger of this fallacy, I argued, perhaps too briefly, that conditions *sufficient* to establish the truth of propositions Hume doubted are *necessary* to propositions he accepted. Professor Wolff apparently interpreted me as saying merely that Kant's premises are also Hume's premises, whereas in fact I said:

> The justification of the principles is not merely that they produce the kind of knowledge Hume doubted; rather, they are, Kant argued, the *necessary* conditions also for *any* connected experience in time... which any sane man, including Hume, would have to grant.[5]

There is an important logical difference here, for affirming a consequent is valid if the antecedent is a necessary condition.

Let K represent a set of propositions accepted by Kant and doubted or denied by Hume; let H represent a set of propositions Hume (and, incidentally, Kant) accepted; let P stand for propositions sufficient to support K (thus P implies K). Kant's answer to Hume is to show that P is necessary to H and that thus H implies K.

In my footnote, I mentioned propositions necessary for the distinction between erroneous and veridical perception as the crucial assumption Hume had to make in order to support the inductive arguments he needed even for his truncated causal explanations. Now, however, I wish to direct attention to a passage which discusses causation in a way which conforms to the logical pattern just proffered; and though Hume is not mentioned, this passage constitutes, in my opinion, Kant's "answer to Hume." The passage, A 195-96 = B 240-41, occurs in the discussions of the third proof of the Second Analogy, and in order to understand it we must see it in the context of this Analogy.

Kant has been arguing that the apprehension of an objective event, in contradistinction to that of an enduring state of affairs, requires a recognition that the representation we call a representation of an event must occur in a fixed position in the order of our representations, for otherwise we would not be able to distinguish the seriality of our representations of enduring states of affairs from the seriality of our representations of an objective sequence of states of affairs, the transition from one to another of which constitutes an event. The order in which I apprehend the representations of events is fixed by the events, whereas the order in which I apprehend representations of enduring states of affairs is fixed by me or by accident. But an order in appearances (objects and events) is one in which one appearance occurs before another or along with it, and this order has a different status from the order of representations, since always one representation occurs before another even when we are representing to ourselves a state of affairs in which one ingredient does not "take place" before another. We are able to decide that a sequence of representations is evidence of a sequence of events only if the order of the representations is such that we believe (rightly or wrongly) that one of the representations must occur before the other. For in that case, we interpret the first representation, call it R_a, as evidence for the event A, and if R_a cannot (we believe) occur after R_b, we think (rightly or wrongly) that B cannot occur before A. Now a condition under which an event B cannot occur before A is that A is a cause of B. Hence the decision that a given representation R_n is a representation of an event is dependent upon the belief (which may be right or wrong) that what R_n represents occurs after what is represented by R_m and could not occur before it. Hence Kant concludes: The experience of something happening is possible only on the assumption that appearances in their succession, that is, appearances as they happen (= events), are determined by the preceding state.[6]

We now come to the application of this analysis to the views of Kant's predecessors, presumably Hume. It is generally assumed, Kant says, (1) that we discover that A is the cause of B by induction from observations of A's regularly preceding B's; and (2) "that this is the way we are first led to construct for ourselves the concept of cause." Hume argued for both these propositions, and we may call (1) the *"Enquiry-thesis"* and (2) the *"Treatise-thesis,"* after the works in which they are most fully and characteristically elaborated.

Kant fully accepts (1). He is in complete agreement with Hume that our knowledge of causal connections between specific events is a posteriori not a priori, synthetic not analytic, inductive not logical, probable not certain. His methods for finding the cause of B are exactly those which Hume prescribed, and the chances of success in this venture, as estimated by Kant and Hume, are very much the same. Kant's first answer to Hume, then, is to agree with him, and to disagree with the rationalists who thought that logical insight into causal connections was possible.

But Kant denies (2). While we can make "logically clear" the conception of the relation of cause to effect only after we have "employed in experience" (as in [1]) the general rule, to wit, that for B to be an event there must have been *some* other event as the condition for its position in a serial, temporal order, "the recognition of the rule, as a condition of the synthetic unity of appearances in time, has been the ground of the experience [of the sequence of A to B] itself."

What does Hume need in order to find that A is the cause of B? For though he challenges the common and the metaphysical interpretation of "cause," he certainly knows how to use it in experience, and he tells us how we do and should use it in order to avoid mistakes that would damage us in practical life.

He needs (a) to know that some impression I is an impression of (or evidence for) an event and not of a state of affairs (like the side of a house); and (b) to find some other impression I' which regularly precedes I and is likewise the impression of an event.[7] Task (b) is the inductive task, and Kant accedes to Hume's arguments in respect to how it is carried out and what the limitations upon it are. But to accomplish (a), Hume has to be able to decide which of the various impressions are impressions of objective events. He never discussed this problem; no one before Kant even saw that it was a problem. Kant's thesis is that (a) cannot be accomplished unless we accept the rule that representations are to be taken as representations of events only if the representations are already thought to have an order fixed by events which are themselves in a fixed temporal order—even if our thought about the specific order be in fact incorrect. (For the Analogies are regulative principles, not constitutive; they tell us where and when to look for causes and substances, and do not guarantee that we will discover them in specific cases.)

To return now to our logical pattern:

K. "Everything that happens, that is, begins to be, presupposes something upon which it follows by rule" (Kant's Second Analogy).

P. Events can be distinguished from objective enduring states of affairs, even though our apprehension of each is serial (the accomplishment of Hume's task [a]).

H. Among events, we find empirically some pairs of similar ones which tend to be repeated, and we then make the inductive judgment: events like the first members of the pairs are causes of events like the second (the accomplishment of Hume's task [b]).

P implies K, by the arguments of the Second Analogy, which give a sufficient reason for K. H implies P, since if events cannot be distinguished, pairs of events cannot be found, and thus P is a necessary condition of H. Hence: H implies P and P implies K, therefore H implies K. That is Kant's answer to Hume.[8]

NOTES

1. E. W. Schipper, "Kant's Answer to Hume's Problem," *Kant-Studien* 53 (1961) 68-74; M. E. Williams, "Kant's Reply to Hume," ibid., 55 (1965), 71-78.

2. *Prolegomena*, Ak. IV, 258.

3. Robert Paul Wolff, *Kant's Theory of Mental Activity* (Cambridge: Harvard University Press, 1963).

4. Wolff, *Kant's Theory*, p. 49.

5. From my Introduction to *Kant's Prolegomena* (New York, Liberal Arts Press, 1951), p. xix, note. The word "necessary" was not italicized in the original text.

6. A paraphrase of part of the last sentence in the paragraph beginning on A 195 = B 240.

7. It is one of the merits of Mrs. Schipper's article that she argues that Hume and Kant are not using "experience" in the same sense; but she carries this point, in my opinion, too far, in arguing that Kant's analysis applies only to scientific and not to "familiar experience." It would have been better for her to argue that Hume has not yet reached "familiar experience" in which he could distinguish events from enduring states of affairs solely on the basis of the (subjective) association of ideas.

8. [This essay originally appeared in *Ratio* 9 (1967), pp. 33-37, copyright Blackwell Publishers Ltd., and is reprinted with permission.]

Kant and the Right of Revolution

Kant's enthusiasm for the French Revolution, the American Revolution, and the Irish efforts to throw off the English yoke is well known. It earned him the unenviable epithet of "the old Jacobin"; though he condemned the excesses of the Reign of Terror and the execution of the King and Queen, these events which turned many of his compatriots against the Revolution and all its works did not make Kant modify his adherence to the principles of the Revolution; and it was even believed that he was to go to Paris as advisor to Sieyès.[1]

When, therefore, in 1793 he sent his essay, *On the Saying: "That may be true in theory but it does not hold in practice,"* to the *Berlinische Monatsschrift*, the editor wrote him with obvious relief: "To speak quite openly, it pleased me all the more since it refuted the rumor (which I had suspected from the start) that you had come out in favor of the ever increasingly repulsive French Revolution, in which the actual freedom of reason and morality and all wisdom in statecraft and legislation are being most shamefully trampled under foot."[2] For this essay of Kant's denies the right of revolution when the editor had reason to believe that Kant would defend it. But what was a relief to Biester, the editor, has been a paradox to others.

How could a man of Kant's probity sympathize with revolutionists and yet deny the right and justification of revolution? I say a man of Kant's probity; for it has been suggested that Kant's condemnation of revolution in his published works was deceptive, a sop to the censor. Of course we cannot disprove this accusation; but while it is not improbable that Kant was intimidated by the censor, I find it incredible, for Kant's actual response to the censor in 1792 was silence, not deception. In 1766, he had written to Moses Mendelssohn, "Although I am absolutely convinced of many things that I shall never have the courage to say, I shall never say anything I do not believe."[3] I think that was as true in the 1790s as in the 1760s; and therefore, I must try to find some other way to explain the apparent inconsistency in Kant's attitudes.

We can understand Biester's delighted surprise in finding in Kant's essay a denial of the right of revolution. Not only had Kant's reputation as a Jacobin spread to Berlin, but also in his *Idea for a Universal History* published nine years earlier, even before the French Revolution, Kant had spoken the hope that "after many reformative revolutions, a universal cosmopolitical condition...will come into being."[4] In fact, one might almost suppose that the conclusion of *Theory and Practice* came as a surprise to Kant himself; for in unpublished notes we find Kant writing that resistance to government may be justified provided some constitutional provision is made—as he believed it was made in England[5]—under which there can be a formal legal finding that the original contract has been broken by the monarch; and even without such a constitutional provision he held in certain cases that revolution is justified:

> Force, which does not presuppose a judgment having the validity of law [*rechtskräftig Urtheil*] is against the law consequently [the people] cannot rebel except in the cases which cannot at all come forward in a civil union, e.g., the enforcement of a religion, compulsion to unnatural sins, assassination, etc., etc.[6]

—and the etceteration is Kant's own. Given what we know of Kant's theory of natural law and of the justification of positive law by reference to it—a theory as susceptible to a Lockean as to a Hobbesian development—it is easy to suppose that Kant could have asserted the right of resistance to a tyrannical government which denied autonomy to the legislation of the citizens. In fact, one of his disciples, August Wilhelm Rehberg, in the following issue of the *Berlinische Monatsschrift*, replied to Kant and drew precisely this conclusion from Kantian premises:

> If a system of a priori demonstrated positive specifications of natural law is applied to the world of men, nothing less than a complete dissolution of present civil constitutions would follow. For according to such a system, only that constitution is valid which accords with the determination of the ideal of reason. In this case, no one of the existing constitutions could stand.... If these constitutions contradict...the first requirements of a rational constitution, the human race is not only permitted, it is required, to destroy these constitutions which are opposed to the original moral law. The form of the constitution of the state is a matter of indifference, so long as complete equality is established; but to establish this, everything else must be sacrificed.— Thus the theory of revolution is a necessary consequence of the physiocratic system.[7]

Kant spurned Rehberg's essay (without specifically mentioning the putative deduction of the right of rebellion),[8] and his tentative justification of the Glorious Revolution of 1688 remained hidden in his notes. In his published works, there is only one halfhearted commendation for revolution (cited above) and one passage (later than the contribution to Biester's journal) which excuses, if it does not justify, revolution. It occurs in the *Rechtslehre*, where Kant speaks of a people's having "at least some excuse for forcibly [dethroning a monarch] by appealing to the right of necessity [which knows no law]."[9] But otherwise Kant's denial of the right of revolution is as firm and clear as his express sympathy for the French Revolution.

I shall proceed to examine this paradox as follows. I shall first state Kant's jurisprudential objections to the right to revolt; next I shall give a brief summary of those parts of his political theory which provide a context for his understanding of the events of 1789; then I shall discuss the non-jurisprudential ground of his sympathy with the Revolution. In conclusion, I shall draw some comparisons between his views and those of Hegel.

1. Kant's argument against the right of revolution is brief to the point of lucidity. By virtue of the ideal of the social contract, sovereignty is indivisible. A constitution cannot have within it a positive law permitting the abrogation of the constitution; there is a contradiction in the conception of a publicly constituted *Gegenmacht.*[10]

> The constitution cannot contain any article that would allow for some authority in the state that could resist or restrain the chief magistrate in cases in which he violates the constitutional laws. For he who is supposed to restrain the authority of the state must have more power than, or at least as much power as, the person whom he is supposed to restrain...; in other words, he must be able to command the resistance publicly. But then the latter would be the chief magistrate, not the former; and this supposition contradicts itself.[11]

> To permit any opposition to this absolute power (an opposition that might limit that supreme authority) would be to contradict oneself, inasmuch as in that case the power (which may be opposed) would not be the lawful supreme authority that determines what is or is not to be publicly just.[12]

In this argument, we see Kant's formalism *in extremis*. There cannot be a law which permits lawlessness, nor an institution of power that provides for its own forcible dissolution.

It seems to me that no one should be unduly shocked by Kant's argument; and if one is not convinced, it is because one objects to the narrowness of Kant's base, not to the stringency of his proof erected upon it. The revolutionist does not appeal to the terms of the constitution for justification of his efforts to overturn the constitution; at most he appeals to the constitution for reform of administrative practices, or perhaps to the preamble of the constitution with its adumbration of natural, not positive, law as a basis for criticism of the positive law and the constitution which he rejects. In the *Rechtslehre*, which is concerned with the a priori foundation of civil society, Kant could have drawn no other conclusion. Revolution abrogates positive law; therefore positive law and its system condemn revolution. Revolution means a return to nature, which the contract establishing positive law renounces.[13]

Up to this point it may appear that Kant is making a point of boring obviousness, namely, that there can be no *legal* right of revolution. Revolution by its very nature is a denial that established legal and constitutional claims are indefeasible; and to tell a revolutionary that he should desist from his revolutionary activity because he is breaking a law would be met with derision.

In *Perpetual Peace*, however, there is another criticism of the putative right of revolution, a criticism which is more deeply rooted in Kant's moral philosophy than in his metaphysics of jurisprudence. The previous argument is, as it were, a legalistic consequence of the categorical imperative in the form which forbids us from acting on maxims which are self-contradictory when universalized. The new argument is derived from the form of the categorical imperative which requires us to treat human beings as end-setting ends in themselves, and it leads to what Kant calls the "transcendental formula of public law": "All actions relating to the right of other men are unjust if their maxim is not consistent with publicity." "The illegitimacy of rebellion," he infers, "is thus clear from the fact that its maxim, if openly acknowledged, would make its own purpose impossible. Therefore [the maxim to revolt on occasion] would have to be kept secret"[14] in order to be effective, and is therefore illegitimate. The maxim to put down revolution, however, passes this test and is likely to be most effective when given the widest publicity.

In place of revolution, Kant favors evolution. The evolution of the state to a more just form and administration, Kant believes, is inevitable only if there is public enlightenment and freedom of the press. The free press is the palladium of human rights.[15] It permits the reform of the state by apprising the rulers of the dissatisfactions of the subjects, and it is to the interests of the rulers themselves that these dissatisfactions be removed, since an irrational legislation—one decided for the people in a way in which the people would not decide for themselves[16]—makes for instability in the government and insecurity of the rulers. Reform can be effected only by the sovereign,[17] but it can be undertaken by him with wisdom only if he is made aware of the inequities and inadequacies of his administration.

Until this reform is effected, however, the people must obey. For to disobey is to return to the state of nature and to leave it to chance, or providence, whether the new government yet to be established will be better or worse than the one which is overthrown. Reform means progress, the metamorphosis of the state; revolution means palingenesis[18] of the state, a new beginning of civil society from the state of nature without profit from the steps previously taken on the path away from the state of nature.

That a government may have been established by an act of lawless violence does not impugn its legal authority and validity, nor reduce its claim to allegiance. Kant is willing to believe that all governments began with power, not with contract. But to inquire into the historical origin of a government for the purpose of thereby impugning its authority is itself punishable.[19] This principle of the irrelevancy of historical origin to judicial validity is used to legitimize the government which is, in point of historical fact, established as a result of insurrection.[20] The new government cannot legitimately punish the fallen ruler, since he could, under the previous constitution, have done no (punishable) wrong.[21]

2. I turn now to Kant's theory of government, in which the doctrine of the separation of powers is the most basic principle.

The sovereign (*Beherrscher*) or lawgiver of a people (the head of the state) derives his rightful authority from the united people under the contract.[22] It is as though he held his legislative authority from the perfect lawgiver, God.[23] But his actual authority is in all probability based upon his power, with only a *post facto* justification of it by the ideal of the contract. The sovereign has rights with respect to the subject, but no coercive duties.[24] Hence the sovereign can do no wrong[25] in the sense that nothing he does is punishable: "There is no right of sedition, much less a right of revolution, and least of all a right to lay hands on or to take the life of the chief of state."[26]

The head of the government (*Regent*) is the agent of the sovereign. His commands are not laws but only ordinances and decrees.[27] He is obligated to the sovereign and subject to the laws given by the sovereign. His decrees must be obeyed by the subjects, and even if he proceeds contrary to the law, the citizens must not actively resist him except by exercising their freedom to criticize and petition for reform.[28] But the head of the government may be deposed by the sovereign and the sovereign may modify his administration.[29]

Various abortive forms of government arise when the legislative, judicial, and executive functions of government are confused or lodged in the same moral or physical person. If the same person both makes and executes the laws—if, that is, the sovereign is himself the head of the government or the supreme judge—the system of checks and balances is not in effect, and the government is despotic.[30] A government may be monarchical in form while republican in spirit if the sovereignty resides in the united people, and the person of the sovereign represents the interests and rights of the people.

The ultimate agency of legitimate reform in the government lies in the person of the sovereign, as we have seen; but there are limits even on his right to change the constitution. The sovereign, for example, cannot validly arrange a transformation of one constitution to another (for example, from an aristocracy to a democracy), for these are matters for only the collective will of the people to decide. "Even if the sovereign were to decide to transform himself into a democracy," Kant writes, "he would be doing the people an injustice, because the people themselves might abhor this kind of constitution and might find that one of the other two was more advantageous to them."[31]

When the chief of state allows himself to be represented in a body of deputies of the people, sovereignty *ipso facto* reverts to the collective people; the surrender of sovereignty by the person of the monarch has already occurred,[32] and it cannot be regained at the end of some specified time unless it is freely granted by the body of the people or their deputies. This event, according to Kant, took place on May 5, 1789, when "the sovereignty of the monarch disappeared completely...and passed over to the people, to whose legislative will the property of every citizen now became subject." What was not justified was, first, the surrender of his sovereignty by Louis XVI to the Estates General; and, second, the execution of the former monarch—an act which "fills the soul, conscious of the ideas of human justice, with horror."[33]

But the success of the Revolution, in spite of the illegitimacy of its beginning and the crimes which marked its effectuation, "binds the subjects to accept the new order of things as good citizens, and they cannot refuse to honor and obey the suzerain (*Obrigkeit*) who now possesses authority."[34]

Kant's fervid denial of the right of revolution, therefore, is historically focused not against the Estates General and the successor government, but upon the efforts at counterrevolution and restoration of the Bourbons. Thus he specifically denounces the right claimed by other sovereigns to intervene in French affairs so as to undo the Revolution.[35]

Our exposition has perhaps let it appear that Kant's formalism—the notion that a legal right to rebel is self-contradictory and a moral right to rebel is unjustifiable—makes him oppose all revolutions yet to come, while precisely the same formalism permits him to accept all successful revolutions of the past, especially those of 1688, 1776, and 1789. His enthusiasm for these revolutions, especially that of 1789, is made compatible with his denial of the right of revolution, for "revolution" now means "Restoration." This, however, would seem to me to be time-serving dishonesty which one would not willingly attribute to Kant if a more ingenuous resolution of the original paradox is possible.

But even if one hesitates to apply to Kant the maxim that what matters is "whose ox is being gored," there is a sophistic legalism in his theory of a non juridical transfer of sovereignty from Louis XVI to the Estates General. He seems to be exculpating the Estates from the charge of rebellion, saying rather that they discharged the duty that legally devolved upon them to "reform" the government. This outcome, to be sure, removes the paradox with which I began this paper: Kant disapproved of revolutions, but what was called the French Revolution was not really a revolution or, if it was a revolution, the only revolutionary was Louis XVI![36] Surely, however, this is explaining away one paradox by means of a greater one.

3. To remove the paradox requires us to consider things not from a moralistic or legalistic point of view, which is perhaps the one most natural to Kant, but from the standpoint of his teleological conception of history. For from this point of view alone can Kant justify comparing a state before and after a revolution and thus pronounce a moral judgment on a revolution unjustified a priori on grounds of positive law and on the natural law that authority must be obeyed.

In so doing, however, Kant cannot, without being unfaithful to his moral principles, appeal to a utilitarian justification for a revolution. And he does not do so;[37] whether a people is happier before or after a revolution is as irrelevant from the standpoint of the judgment of the philosophy of history as it is from the standpoint of positive or moral law. Progress in history is not measured by the happiness of the people but by the formal criterion of the rule of law and the scope of juridical freedom.

The perfect civic constitution, Kant holds, is republican, for it alone derives from the idea of the original compact which is the norm, if not the historical genesis, of all government:

> The republican constitution is the only enduring political constitution
> in which the law is autonomous and is not annexed to any particular
> person. It is the ultimate end of all public law and the only condition

under which each person receives his due peremptorily.... [Under any other form of government] it must be recognized that only a provisory internal justice and no absolutely juridical state of civil society can exist.[38]

The republican constitution is with respect to the law the one which is the original basis of every form of civil constitution.[39]

Thus Kant can distinguish between revolutions toward the better and revolutions toward the worse, though *qua* revolution both are to be condemned. Since revolution produces an *interregnum* which is equivalent to the state of nature, revolutions probably have a tendency to end in a worse government than the government which could have been achieved by gradual reform. Political wisdom, therefore, stands on the side of reform to make the constitution better accord with the ideal of law; but "when nature herself produces revolutions," political wisdom will use them "as a call of nature for fundamental reforms to produce a lawful constitution founded upon principles of freedom, for only such a constitution is durable."[40]

When nature herself produces revolutions...! The *Idea for a Universal History* is like a theodicy, asking "Is it reasonable to assume a purposiveness in all the parts of nature and to deny it to the whole?"[41] Kant answers: "The history of mankind can be seen, in the large, as the realization of Nature's secret plan to bring forth a perfectly constituted state."[42] The unsocial sociability of mankind, the competition among tribes and states which leads to war, and revolutions—all of which are judged, juridically and moralistically, to be evil—are the means nature uses in realizing her "secret plan" for mankind.

That the French Revolution is to be understood at least by analogy to natural teleology is made clear in the *Critique of Judgment*. The organization of nature, Kant tells us, has nothing analogous to any causality known to us, but it throws light on "a complete transformation, recently undertaken, of a great people into a state" where

the word "organization" has frequently, and with much propriety, been used for the constitution of the legal authorities and even of the entire body politic. For in a whole of this kind certainly no member should be a mere means, but should also be an end, and, seeing that he contributes to the possibility of the entire body, should have his position and function in turn defined by the idea of the whole.[43]

But the French Revolution is not to be understood only by analogy to natural teleology; it has a distinctively moral dimension too. In the *Strife of the Faculties*, Kant draws a moral conclusion from the French Revolution. The passionate participation in the good, namely, the disinterested enthusiasm with which the Revolution was greeted, could have no other cause, Kant thinks, than a moral predisposition in the human race to seek what is ideal and purely moral.[44]

It gives hope and evidence of the moral progress of mankind. The participants in the Revolution, of course, were not morally disinterested; but the impartial spectators approved, and "such a phenomenon in human history"—Kant is not now speaking of the Revolution, but of the moral enthusiasm it engendered—"is *not to be forgotten*, for it revealed a tendency and faculty in human nature for improvement such as no politician, affecting wisdom, might have conjured out of the course of things hitherto existing, and one which nature and freedom alone, united in the human race in conformity with inner principles of right, could have promised."[45]

4. Kant does not have a categorial scheme adequate to take account of the juxtaposition of the illegality and immorality of a man who makes a revolution and what might be called his higher morality when, through revolutionary activity, he establishes a better stage of political culture as a basis for further moral development. He does not accept the doing of evil that good may result. He does not do so in part because his political ethics reduces to the maxim of my station and its duties except insofar as complaining and striving to reform a government are imprescriptible rights; and in part because his conception of natural law is static.[46] Not only is it static; it is in fact inconsistent, for it includes both the teleology of seeking to bring about the rule of law under a republican constitution (which may, in fact, require not merely efforts at reform but actual violence[47]) and a formalism of obedience to the powers that be. The duty we have to contribute to the progress of mankind is a duty of imperfect obligation, is unenforceable, and leaves elbowroom for its realization. The latter, the duty we have to fulfill the requirements of the established law, is a duty of strict or perfect obligation, and is thus for Kant prior in its claims to the former.[48] As consequences of this priority of duties of perfect over duties of imperfect obligation are those famous cases which have served for generations as a *reductio ad absurdum* of Kantian ethics, for example, the denial of the right to lie in order to save the life of an innocent man. A like consequence is here drawn in Kant's political philosophy. We are to work toward the end of the improvement of mankind by striving to secure a political stage on which the rights of man will be respected and war will be abolished. But in so doing, we are not to overthrow by violence even a tyrannical government which blatantly traduces these rights. for to do this would conflict with a duty of perfect obligation. We are not, therefore, justified in killing a tyrant in order to preserve the lives of thousands or millions of his subjects. The most I can morally do is to expose the abuses of his power and make proposals for his reform, to disobey him if he commands me to do something immoral and to suffer martyrdom if necessary.[49]

A conception of natural law which is evolutionary can profit from an understanding of the inconsistency into which Kant falls in condemning revolution while holding that the enthusiasm for the French Revolution sprang from a moral disposition in mankind. The moral aspirations of mankind are not satisfied by punctilious obedience to the powers that be; they demand that the powers that be should earn our respectful obedience, and they sometimes justify the disobedience to the positive law out of obedience to a "higher law." Both obligations are rational and natural, and it takes deep moral and historical insight to adjudicate their conflict, and this adjudication need not and does not always lead to the same decision. An evolutionary view of morality and of the law of nature draws a distinction between the morality of stable societies, which is necessary to maintain or to gradually improve the status quo, and the historical demands which abrogate static laws and institutions when they fall significantly below the level of moral aspiration; but no rules can be given for this adjudication which will decree an all-or-none answer in periods threatened by, or promised, radical changes.

The agents whose acts are directed against the stable moral order are, descriptively, criminals; but they may be, in Hegel's terms, men whose "words and deeds are the best of the age."[50] If they succeed, their words and ideas will be the ruling words and ideas of the new moral community they will produce—and if they fail, they will (rightly) be hanged as common criminals against the stable ethical order.

Such an evolutionary conception—an evolutionary conception which is meant to justify revolution, if that is what is required for progress—is found in Hegel's dialectic of private morals (*Moralität*), public ethics (*Sittlichkeit*), and the egotism of world-historical individuals whose crimes against the first two are converted, by the cunning of world-reason, into quantum jumps in the moral progress of the community or state:

> The basis of duty is the civil life: the individuals have their assigned business and hence their assigned duties. Their morality consists in acting accordingly.... But each individual is also the child of a people at a definite state of its development.... A moral whole [a specific moral community], as such, is limited. It must have above it a higher universality, which makes it disunited with itself. The transition from one spiritual pattern to the next is just this, that the former moral whole is abolished.... It is at this point that appear those momentous collisions between existing acknowledged duties, laws, and rights, and those possibilities which are adverse to this system, violate it, and even destroy its foundations and existence.... These possibilites now become historical fact; they involve a universal of an order different from that upon which the permanence of a people or a state depends. This universal is an essential phase in the development of the creating Idea, of truth striving and urging towards itself.[51]

Thus arises the conflict between the morally good man who fulfills the duty of his station and the man who breaks down that system—the "world-historical individual" who is impudently judged to be immoral by schoolmasters and valets, "those exquisite discerners of spirits."

But the history of the world moves on a higher level than that proper to morality.... Those who, through moral steadfastness and noble sentiment, have resisted the necessary progress of the Spirit stand higher in moral value than those whose crimes have been turned by a higher order into means of carrying on the will behind this order.... They stand outside morality. The litany of the private virtues of modesty, humility, love, and charity must not be raised against them.[52]

This is a teleological suspension of the ethical, to adapt Kierkegaard's terminology to a new use.

Kant's enthusiasm for the French Revolution is based upon his teleological conception of history, which is a forerunner of Hegel's definition of history as "the progress of the consciousness of freedom." That the final purpose of the world is moral, not eudaemonistic, makes it possible for Kant to have a moral enthusiasm for the Revolution which his formalistic moral system does not justify. Had Kant's approval of the Revolution been eudaemonistic, the inconsistency would have been greater. But some inconsistency remains because Kantian ethics is not adequate to resolve the painful problems of conflicting duties.[53, 54]

NOTES

1. An account of this rumor will be found in G. P. Gooch, *Germany and the French Revolution* (London, 1920), pp. 276-77.

2. Biester to Kant, Oct. 5, 1792 (Ak. XI, 456; Zweig, *Correspondence*, pp. 208-09).

3. Letter to Mendelssohn, April 8, 1766 (Ak. X, 69; Zweig, *Correspondence*, p. 54).

4. Ak. VIII, 28; *Kant on History*, ed. L. W. Beck (Indianapolis, 1963), p. 23. The words translated "reformative revolutions" (*Revolutionen der Umbildung*) do not suggest (as the English words may) that these revolutions were to be bloodless.

5. Reflexionen 8043, 8044; Ak. XIX, 590, 591. But popular violence (*turbas*) is forbidden. In *Über den Gemeinspruch: Das mag in der Theorie richtig sein, taugt aber nicht für die Praxis* (Ak. VIII, 303; *On the Old Saw: That May Be Right in Theory but It Won't Work in Practice*, trans. E. B.Ashton [University of Pennsylvania Press, 1974], p. 71), he approves of the silence of the "contractual arrangement" made in 1688 with respect to the right to overthrow a monarch who does not fulfill it.

6. Reflexion 8051; Ak. XIX, 594-95. The passages cited by H. S. Reiss ("Kant and the Right of Rebellion," *Journal of the History of Ideas* 17 [1956], 190-91) as evidence that Kant justified seeking to overthrow government under the saying, "We ought to obey God rather than men" (*Religion innerhalb der Grenzen der bloßen Vernunft*, Ak. VI, 99 n.; trans. Greene and Hudson, p. 90 n.) do not seem to me to go beyond the justification of passive disobedience, and not even to go that far when the politico-civil law does not command anything "in itself evil."

7. *Über das Verhältnis der Theorie zur Praxis* (1793), in *Über Theorie und Praxis*, ed. Dieter Henrich (Suhrkamp, 1967), p. 128.

8. Letter to Biester, April 10, 1794 (Ak. XI, 496-97; not in Zweig).

9. *Rechtslehre* (Part I of *Metaphysik der Sitten*), Ak. VI, 321 n.; cf. 236; *Metaphysical Elements of Justice*, trans. John Ladd (Indianapolis, 1965), p. 87 n.; cf. p. 42.

10. *Über den Gemeinspruch*, Ak. VIII, 303 (Ashton, p. 71).

11. *Rechtslehre*, Ak. VI, 319 (Ladd, p. 85).

12. Ibid., Ak. VI, 372 (Ladd, pp. 140-41).

13. Ibid., Ak. VI, 355 (Ladd, p. 129).

14. *Zum ewigen Frieden*, Ak. VIII, 381; in *Kant on History*, pp. 129-30.

15. *Über den Gemeinspruch*, Ak. VIII, 304 (Ashton, p. 72).

16. *Rechtslehre*, Ak. VI, 327 (Ladd, p. 95).

17. Ibid., Ak. VI, 321-22 (Ladd, p. 88).

18. Ibid., Ak. VI, 339-40 (Ladd, p. 111).

19. Ibid., Ak. VI, 319, 339-40, 372 (Ladd, pp. 84, 111, 140).

20. Ibid., Ak. VI, 323 (Ladd, p. 89).

21. Ibid., Ak. VI, 317, 341 (Ladd, pp. 82, 113-14).

22. Ibid., Ak. VI, 315 (Ladd, p. 80).

23. Ibid., Ak. VI, 319 (Ladd, pp. 84-85).

24. Ibid., Ak. VI, 319, cf. 241 (Ladd, p. 85, cf. p. 47).

25. Ibid., Ak. VI, 317 (Ladd, p. 82).

26. Ibid., Ak. VI, 320 (Ladd, p. 86).

27. Ibid., Ak. VI, 317 (Ladd, p. 82).

28. Ibid., Ak. VI, 319 (Ladd, p. 85).

29. Ibid., Ak. VI, 317, 321-22 (Ladd, pp. 82, 88).

30. Ibid., Ak. VI, 317, 319 (Ladd, pp. 82, 85).

31. Ibid., Ak. VI, 340 (Ladd, p. 113).

32. Ibid., Ak. VI, 341 (Ladd, p. 113). The King had plenty of warning against con-voking the Estates General, with such admonitions as "Un roi qui subit une Constitution se croit dégradé: un Roi qui propose une Constitution obtient la plus belle gloire qui soit parmi les hommes...." and besides "It is illegal!" (see Jean Egret, *La Pré-révolution française* [Paris, 1961], p. 322, and George Lefebvre, *The Coming of the French Revolution* [New York, 1959], p. 27). But the notion that it was radically "unconstitutional" (like an act of revolution itself) seems to be original with Kant. More study of the polemical literature of the time, however, might reveal earlier sources for this singular idea.

33. *Rechtslehre*, Ak. VI, 321 n. (Ladd, p. 87 n.). There is, however, an inconsistency in Kant's comparing the execution of Louis XVI to an act of state suicide, since it follows from his thesis that Louis was no longer sovereign. He suffered injustice, to be sure, and one can sympathize with Kant's abhorrence of this act without putting it into a special class "more heinous than murder itself," inexplicable except as "the pure Idea of extreme perversity" (Ak. 322 n.; Ladd, p. 88 n.).

34. Ibid., Ak. VI, 323 (Ladd, p. 89).

35. *Zum ewigen Frieden*, Ak. VIII, 346 (*Kant On History*, p. 89).

36. Cf. Dieter Henrich, "Einleitung," *Theorie und Praxis*, p. 32.

37. *Rechtslehre*, Ak. VI, 318 (Ladd, p. 83).

38. Ibid., Ak. VI, 341 (Ladd, pp. 112-13).

39. *Zum ewigen Frieden*, Ak. VIII, 350 (*Kant on History*, p. 94).

40. Ibid., Ak. VIII, 373 n. (*Kant on History*, p. 120 n.).

41. *Idee zu einer allgemeinen Geschichte in weltbürgerlicher Absicht*, Ak. VIII, 25 (*Kant on History*, p. 20).

42. Ibid., Ak. VIII, 27 (*Kant on History*, p. 21).

43. *Critique of Judgment*, Ak. V, 375 n. (*Critique of Teleological Judgment*, trans. J. C. Meredith [Oxford, 1952], p. 23 n.).

44. *Der Streit der Fakultäten*, Ak. VII, 85-86 (*Kant on History*, pp. 144-45).

45. Ibid., Ak. VII, 88 (*Kant on History*, p. 147).

46. Not natural law, of course, in the sense that the study of empirical nature gives rise to it; it is a law of reason. But it functions in the same way as natural law, as a norm and warrant for positive law. See Leonard Krieger, "Kant and the Crisis in Natural Law," *Journal of the History of Ideas* 26 (1965), 191-210, esp. 201, 207.

47. As certainly the first step from a state of natural savagery to civil society required the exercise of a natural right to violence: "Everyone may use violent means to compel another to enter into a juridical state of society" (*Rechtslehre*, Ak. VI, 312; Ladd pp. 76-77).

48. *Zum ewigen Frieden*, Ak. VII, 377 (*Kant on History*, p. 124).

49. *Critique of Practical Reason*, Ak. V, 155-56 (trans. L. W. Beck [New York, 1956], 159 f.), on the effort of Henry VIII to suborn a witness against Ann Boleyn.

50. *Die Vernunft in der Geschichte (Einleitung in die Philosophie der Welt-geschichte), Sämmtliche Werke*, ed. G. Lasson (Leipzig, 1930), VIII, 76 (*Reason in History*, trans. R. S. Hartman [Indianapolis, 1953], p. 40).

51. Ibid., 73-75 (Hartman [slightly modified], pp. 38-39). No inferences must be drawn, of course, from this passage concerning Hegel's own view of the right of revolution and, specifically, the French Revolution; much else entered into his judgment on these questions. I have dealt with this topic in detail in "The Reformation, the Revolution, and the Restoration in Hegel's Political Philosophy," *Journal of the History of Philosophy* 14 (1976), 51-61.

52. Ibid., 153, 154 (Hartman, p. 82; trans. slightly modified).

53. He even denies that conflicts of duties exist. *Metaphysik der Sitten, Einleitung*, Ak. VI, 224 (Ladd, p. 25).

54. [This essay originally appeared in the *Journal of the History of Ideas* 32 (1971), pp. 411-22, and is reprinted with permission.]

Did the Sage of Königsberg Have No Dreams?

This question was asked by C. I. Lewis[1] in order to show that Kant demanded too much of his categories. According to Lewis, Kant required his categories to limit experience to what is categorizable and to prevent us from having non-categorizable experiences. Lewis, on the other hand, wanted to leave experience independent of the categories, and to use categories not as a dam against an otherwise uncontrollable flood of experiences but as nets with which to capture some experiences which, for that very reason, will be taken as referring to objects. "A priori principles of categorial interpretation," he writes, "are required to limit *reality*; they are not required to limit *experience*."[2] Dreams and illusions are experienced, but they are not caught by our normal categorial net; hence they are not taken to be real. But according to Lewis's interpretation of Kant, Kant could not account for even the *awareness* of dreams and illusions, since Kantian categories would keep us from being conscious of them.

My purpose today is to find out how Kant would have defended the obvious answer to Lewis's penetrating question.

In §13 of the *Critique of Pure Reason* Kant points out a "difficulty" in justifying the necessary objective validity of concepts which do not arise by abstraction from intuitions.

> The categories of the understanding...do not represent conditions under which objects are given in intuition. Objects may, therefore, appear to us without their being under the necessity of being related to the functions of understanding, and understanding, therefore, need not contain their a priori conditions.... Appearances might very well be so constituted that the understanding should not find them to be in accordance with the principles of its unity. Everything might be in such confusion, for instance, in the series of appearances that nothing presented itself which might yield a rule of synthesis and so answer to the conception of cause and effect.[3]

This famous and puzzling passage has caused "astonishment and even indignation"[4] among commentators. There are two competing interpretations. According to the "patchwork theory," when Kant wrote it he believed that these sentences might be true, and had not yet found an argument to show that they were not.[5] According to the other, this possibility was entertained only pedagogically; Kant was asking a question which he imagined his readers would naturally ask and was preparing them for an argument by which this "difficulty" could be averted.[6] Both interpretations agree that Kant finally denied the possibility left open in §13, and only differ about whether he had ever positively affirmed it. If he did really affirm it, at that time he had a simple answer to Lewis's question; and the more the *Critique* moves away from it, the more exposed it is to the scorn of the argument from dreams.

Let us see how Kant removed the "difficulty" of §13, and see if he still left himself a way to admit that he did have dreams. We must draw two distinctions which are implicit in the *Critique* but which are never made explicit.

TWO MEANINGS OF "EXPERIENCE"

Lewis says that Kant used the word "experience" "as if experience and the phenomenally real [i.e., the objectively valid] coincide."[7] Sometimes he did so, sometimes not. The opening sentences of the Introductions to both editions use the word "experience" equivocally. In B we read:

> There can be no doubt that all our knowledge begins with experience. For [otherwise] how should our faculty of knowledge...work up the raw material of sensible impressions into that knowledge of objects which is called experience?[8]

In the first sentence, "experience" means "the raw material of sensible impressions," the manifold of apprehensions or Lockean ideas without the conceptual and interpretative activities of the mind. In the second sentence "experience" means "knowledge of objects" and does perhaps, in Lewis's expression, "coincide with the phenomenally real." Let us call these two meanings "Lockean experience" and "Kantian experience," or, for short, L-experience and K-experience.

One way of reading the *Critique of Pure Reason* is to see it as an answer to the question: how do we move from L-experience to K-experience? And if this were the whole truth about the *Critique*, Kant would have a simple answer to Lewis's question: we make this move with only partial success. This is, briefly, Lewis's *own* answer.

TWO MEANINGS OF "INTUITION"

The *Critique* begins with an inspectional conception of intuition and ends with a functional conception. According to the first, an intuition is a passively received inspectable sensory datum giving consciousness of an individual object independently of all categorization. It is given to consciousness as it were ready-made and labeled. The following examples show this usage:

> In whatever manner and by whatever means a cognition may be related to objects, intuition is that through which it is in immediate relation to them.[9]

> Intuition relates immediately to the object and is single.[10]

> Appearances [= representations] are the sole objects which can be
> given to us immediately, and that in them which relates immediately
> to the object is called intuition.[11]

The inspectional conception of intuition is presupposed in the "difficulty" raised
in §13. Given this conception of intuition, it is obvious that there could be intuitions which would not be tractable to categorial rules.[12]

The development of the functional conception of intuition is Kant's way of
resolving the "difficulty." This development represents the shift from a
pre-Copernican to a Copernican conception of the relation of knowledge to object. Kant substitutes for the unknowable relation of representations to ontologically independent objects the rule-governed relation of representations to each
other. This brings a new conception of object, and with it a new, a functional
conception of intuition.

The new conception of object:

> In so far as our cognitions are to relate to an object, they must neces-
> sarily agree with one another, that is, must possess that unity which
> constitutes the concept of an object.[13]

> Appearance, in contradistinction to the [mere] representations of ap-
> prehension, can be represented as an object distinct from them only if
> it stands under a rule which distinguishes it from every other appre-
> hension and necessitates one particular mode of connection of the
> manifold [of apprehension]. The object is that in the appearance
> which contains the condition of this necessary rule of apprehension.[14]

The object is that the concept of which is a rule for the synthesis of representations which, by conformity to that concept, are descriptive of it or serve as evidence for its existence.

And the new conception of intuition:

> The fact that this affection of sensibility [sc. intuition] is in me does
> not amount to a relation of such representation to any object.[15]

> Thought is the act which relates given intuition to an object.[16]

Note how radically the second sentence contradicts the inspectional conception.
According to this, the pattern was:

$$\text{concept} \rightarrow \text{intuition} \rightarrow \text{object}$$

According to the last quotation, the pattern now is:

$$\text{intuition} \rightarrow \text{concept} \rightarrow \text{object}.$$

On the inspectional view, there could be intuitions which relate immediately to objects but do not conform to the categories; representations might not be synthesizable or constructable under the concept of the object and could belong only to L-experience. According to the functional view, representations which do not conform to the concept of the object may be experienced but are not considered intuitions precisely because they fail to conform to the concept of the object.

If this were the whole truth, Kant could easily explain to Lewis how he dreamt. In fact, if this were the whole answer, it would have been so obvious that Lewis would never have raised the question, for Kant would have anticipated Lewis's most original contribution to the theory of categories.

Important as these two distinctions are, they seem nevertheless to be inconsistent with the central line of thought of the *Critique* (which does seem to give Kant difficulties with Lewis's question). This line of thought is the *nervus probandi* of the Transcendental Deduction, which I shall try to compress into four premises and a conclusion.

> 1. The "I think" must be able to accompany all of my representations of which I am conscious.[17]
> 2. To think is to judge.[18]
> 3. To judge is to relate representations to one another according to a rule given by a category.[19]
> 4. Representations synthetically related to each other according to the rule given by a category as a concept of an object in general are the same as representations related to objects.[20]
> 5. Therefore, relation to an object must be ascribed to all representations of which we are conscious.[21]

As a result of this argument, Kemp Smith concluded:

> Only in and through relation to an object can sense-representations be apprehended.... Relation to an object is constituted by the categories, because only thereby is consciousness of any kind possible at all.[22]

From this it follows for Kemp Smith that L-experience is not conscious experience, that animals are not conscious, and, presumably, that dreams are not possible. While Kemp Smith does not always adhere to these shocking conclusions, he describes the position I have just quoted as the "truly Critical position" to which Kant moved when he escaped from the "difficulty" pointed out in §13. What to Kemp Smith appeared "the truly Critical position" appeared to Lewis, however, to be an absurdity which could be exposed by his flippant question.

Through an exhaustive collection of texts Paton showed that Kant did not draw any of these conclusions from the Transcendental Deduction.[23] But while this was historically interesting, it did not show that Kant *ought not* to have drawn them or how he avoided drawing them. This is what I propose to show.

In one of his private notes Kant added to the first premise another statement which, had it been explicitly stated in the *Critique*, would have made the transcendental deduction less clear. He wrote:

> Consciousness can accompany all representations, *and thus also those of imagination*, which, and the play of which, is itself an object of *inner* sense, and of which it must be possible to become conscious as such an object.[24]

We shall work our way slowly to a justification of this addendum; but first of all we need to see whether the radical Kemp Smith-Lewis conclusions truly follow from the statement of the transcendental deduction in its restricted, classical form. I shall argue that they do not, and thus that Kant could, without inconsistency, have made the addendum in the *Critique* itself.

Kant does not anywhere say that the "I think" must accompany all of my representations; he says merely that it must be able to accompany them. While there is no representation, presumably, which cannot be judgingly related to the rest, it does not follow from Kant's statement that every representation is in fact judged to be related to the rest. A perception that *could not* be accompanied by "I think" "would not belong to any experience, consequently would be without an object, merely a blind play of representations, less even than a dream."[25] While the words "without an object" suggest that K-experience is meant, the last phrase of the sentence shows that L-experience is meant also. I could not even be aware of a representation of which I could not say "I think it," for such a representation would be "nothing to me," [26] "nothing at all,"[27] "less even than a dream."[28] It would not only not represent an object; "I would not even be able to know that I have [it]."[29]

This modification weakens the claim made in the conclusion, which should now read:

> 5'.   Relation to an object must be *ascribable* to every representation of which we are conscious.

This conclusion, however, is rejected by Kant because he holds that some representations have no possible objective reference.[30] The conclusion he wants to draw, and which he does draw in the Refutation of Idealism in B, is:

> 5".   Relation to an object must be *ascribed* to *some* representations of which we are conscious.

The argument of the Refutation of Idealism is that we do not start with an awareness of subjective representations (L-experience) and subsequently infer that some of them have objective reference. Rather, awareness of the subjective stream of consciousness is cognate with the awareness of the non-self or object.[31] Without the representations of outer sense or spatial intuition we have no conception of an inner nonspatial subjective realm of *mere* representations. I cannot say of one representation that it is merely a modification of *my mind* unless I can say of some other representations that they stand for objects; I cannot be conscious of myself except in so far as I am conscious of what is not-self.

The Refutation of Idealism does not require of any particular outer experience that it be veridical: I can dream of Paris as well as see Paris, and

> the difference between truth and dreaming is not ascertained by the nature of the representations which are referred to objects (for they are the same in the two cases) but by their connection according to those rules which determine the coherence of the representations in the concept of an object, and by ascertaining whether they can subsist together in [K-] experience or not.[32]

Outer representations

> can very well be the product merely of the imagination (as in dreams and illusions). Such representation is merely the reproduction of previous outer perceptions which...are possible only through the reality of outer objects.[33]

Kant is here saying that L-experience is possible only if K-experience is possible; but that there is L-experience (such as dreams and wild sense-data) which is not taken up into K-experience. What is not so taken up nevertheless belongs to the consciousness which must contain veridical representations of objects, and may be seen as modifications of my mind and thus as contributing to knowledge of the self as phenomenon of the inner sense. The subjective or empirical unity of apperception, which is my awareness of myself, is dependent upon the transcendental or objective unity of apperception;[34] but I can synthesize all perceptions "in one consciousness of my state"[35] even when I cannot synthesize all of them into consciousness of one world.[36] Thus we reach the justification of the addendum which, we noted, Kant made to the first premise in his private notes, namely the assertion that the "I think" must be able to accompany *all* my representations, whether they be of outer objects or of objects of inner sense.

You may have noticed that the passages which I have been quoting as making it difficult for Kant to explain how we can be aware of what is not conceptualized have been taken largely from the first edition, and the passages quoted as indicating his answer have been taken largely from the second. It is as if someone read the first edition and asked him, "Herr Professor, do you never dream and never have experiences you cannot relate to objects?". In fact, we can date this apocryphal question. It must have been before the *Prolegomena*, and the first answer he gave in §§18-20 of that work was on the level of argument attained in §13 of the *Critique* but surpassed in the later parts of the *Critique*. For this reason most Kant scholars regard this part of the *Prolegomena* as inconsistent with Kant's mature view and cite in support of this the fact that its teachings are not repeated in the second edition of the *Critique*.[37] But we shall see, I hope, that the passages in the *Prolegomena* can be given a sympathetic interpretation which is consistent with what has been said before.

Kant's distinction between judgments of perception and judgments of experience is analogous to that between L-experience and K-experience.[38] Judgments of perception are "only subjectively valid" and require no category.[39] They obtain "reference to an object" through "superadding" a category which is a rule that "they must agree among themselves" and thus have universal, that is to say, objective, validity. Some judgments of perception, for example, "When the sun shines on the stone it becomes warm," can be converted into judgments of experience, for example, "The sun warms the stone," which make no reference to the contingencies of the matter in which *I* happen to have apprehended the event. But there are other judgments of perception, for example, "The room is warm, sugar sweet, wormwood bitter" which "refer only to feeling, which everyone knows to be merely subjective and can of course never be attributed to the object and can never become objective."[40]

There are at least three reasons to be suspicious of Kant's account of judgments of perception, and to regard it more as a statement of a problem, like the "difficulty" of §13 of the *Critique*, than as a permanent part of the edifice of the critical philosophy.

JUDGMENT ALWAYS MAKES A CLAIM TO OBJECTIVITY

Kant writes in the *Critique*:

> I have never been able to accept the interpretations which logicians give of judgment in general. It is, they declare, the representation of a relation between two concepts.[41]

This does not adequately distinguish between a mere association of ideas and a judgment. A judgment is indeed a representation of the relation between concepts, but this does not tell us "in what the asserted relation consists." Kant finds that

> a judgment is nothing but the manner in which given cognitions [intuitions and concepts] are brought to the objective unity of appercep-

tion. This is what is intended by the copula "is." It is employed to distinguish the objective unity of given representations from the subjective. It indicates their relation to the original apperception, and its necessary unity.[42]

But in a judgment of perception "I merely compare perceptions and connect them in a consciousness of my particular state"; the judgment of perception is "merely a connection of perceptions in my mental state, without reference to the object."[43] Since, according to the teaching of the *Critique*, "reference to object" is reduced to "necessary relation of representations among themselves according to a categorial concept," and this necessary relation is what is intended by the objective claim registered by use of the copula, it follows that a judgment of perception as defined in the *Prolegomena* is not a judgment at all as defined in the *Critique*.

It remains to inquire which of the two accounts of judgment is correct, and I suggest that the view of the *Critique* ought to prevail, not only exegetically but also philosophically.

There is a right way and a wrong way to make a judgment of perception. Even a judgment of perception is under rules. While the judgment, "When I see the sun shining on the stone I feel the stone's becoming warm"[44] may be true only *of me*, it is not true merely *for me*. It does not say that if *you* see the one *you* will feel the other; but it does say that *you would be right* if you affirmed that when *I* see the one *I* feel the other, and wrong if you denied it. The judgment is subjective in content (it is perhaps about my subjective L-experience) but objective in its claim to your credence.

In such a judgment I am indeed judging about *my* representations as episodes or states in *my* mental history, and not about what objects these representations may represent. But the *Critique* makes room even for this with the generous scope it allows the term "object": "Everything, every representation even, in so far as we are conscious of it, may be entitled object,"[45] and hence may be judged.

JUDGMENT ALWAYS MAKES USE OF CATEGORIAL CONCEPTS

A judgment does not have to mention a categorial concept, but it has to use one. "The cause of the stone's becoming warm is the sun's shining on it" *mentions* the concept of cause; "the sun warms the stone" *uses* it. Kant seems to think that the judgment, "When the sun shines on the stone, it becomes warm," does neither. He is wrong, or at least inconsistent with the teachings of the *Critique* when he thinks this. The knowledge of the objective succession of sun-shining/stone-becoming-warm requires, according to the Second Analogy, the causal principle. More obviously, "sun" and "stone" are names of substances which are borrowed from external objective experience to denote mere representations. Most obviously, if all even tacit reference to objects were excluded

from the judgment of perception, the mathematical categories would still apply
to the intensive magnitude of the brightness I see when I look at the sun and of
the warmth I feel when I touch the stone. The Anticipation of Perception applies
even to the data of L-experience.[46]

JUDGMENTS PREDICATING SECONDARY QUALITIES OF OBJECTS CAN BE OBJECTIVELY VALID

Kant denies this when he holds "The room is warm" to be a judgment of
perception that can never become a judgment of experience because "it refers
only to feeling."[47] Kant's position here is more extreme than Locke's, but it is
not as consistently held.[48] We must try to work out a consistent view which Kant
did hold at least sometimes.

Let us put one of his judgments of perception into the Theaetetan mode:
"This room feels warm (to me)." This judgment does not ascribe a one-place
predicate to the room. The warmth, grammatically predicated of the room, exists
only in me or in relation to me. The judgment is valid (true) *for me* in the sense
that it is claimed to be true *of me*. Yet this judgment is objectively valid, for the
equivalent judgment, "The room feels warm to Beck," is a judgment of experience about which others can have evidence and on which they must agree if it is
true. What just *I* feel is not part of K-experience; but that I feel what no one else
may feel, for example, the uncomfortable warmth of my fever, is a part of
K-experience.

If my three criticisms of Kant's views in the *Prolegomena* are sound, we
can conclude that judgments of perception are not mere associations of ideas
without objective validity. They may be about associations of ideas, but if correct they are correct for everyone. They report about subjective episodes or
states of mind, and such judgments are made under the rules of the categories.
There is no difficulty in showing then how Kant can be conscious of them. Such
judgments do not belong in K-experience about objects like the sun, the stone,
sugar, and wormwood—what Kant calls objects of the outer sense supposed to
be really existent, and what Prauss calls "objective objects." But they may be
objective in the genuine Kantian sense of being made according to categorial
rules which exact credence from every knowing subject, even if they are about
what Kant calls objects of the inner sense or mere feelings, or what Prauss calls
"subjective objects."[49]

A dream is a subjective object. In a dream I dreamingly-see a three-headed
monster. To dreamingly-see it, unlike to-see-it-*sans-phrase*, does not imply that
there *is* a three-headed monster. But I say, "Last night I dreamt I saw a three-
headed monster," and my judgment about *that* event is as objective as the judgment that I slept in my bed and makes just as valid a claim on your credence.
You cannot verify it by inspection, but the occurrence of the dream, unlike the
monster in the dream, falls under the Second Postulate of Empirical Thought,
fulfilling the criteria of existence. I can verify it by self-observation, and though

I get no knowledge of three-headed monsters, I do get knowledge of myself: Inner sense "represents to consciousness even our own self, only as we appear to ourselves, not as we are in ourselves," but in that respect I am in the same epistemological boat as the three-headed monster (if he really exists and I really see him, not dreamingly-see him).

Lewis, it seems to me, would be in agreement with much of what I profess to have found in Kant. "What is not reality of one sort is reality of another," Lewis writes. "What we do not understand in one way, we shall understand in another. The subsumption of the given under the heading 'dream' or 'illusion' is itself a categorial interpretation by which we understand certain experiences."[50] What we do not know as objective objects we can know as subjective objects. Lewis is using the term "categorial interpretation," however, in a much broader sense than Kant would sanction. The difference between seeing Paris and dreaming that one sees Paris is not a categorial difference, but an empirical difference. The "category" *dream* rightly does not appear in Kant's table. The categories Kant is interested in are presupposed in our having and reporting either type of awareness. The categories do not differentiate veridical from non-veridical experience; they make the difference between dumbly facing chaos without even knowing it—"less even than a dream"[51]—and telling a connected story, even if it is false.

In a lecture on Kant in homage to Milton Nahm I thought it would be inappropriate not to say something about the work of Kant's which Milton Nahm has called "perhaps the most influential writing upon philosophy of art produced in modern times."[52] The *Critique of Judgment*, to the elucidation of which Mr. Nahm has made signal contributions, just had to be referred to for this personal reason. I feared, however, that there was no other reason, and that the artificiality of any device used to make it seem relevant would be obvious to all. Imagine my delighted surprise, therefore, when careful re-reading of the third *Critique* made a real contribution to my working out of the problem before us.

Kant tells us in the *Prolegomena* that "the only reason for the judgments of other men necessarily agreeing with mine [is] the unity of the object" of which each man has the same concept no matter how diverse his sensations.[53] Furthermore, Kant tells us repeatedly, pleasure and displeasure are exclusively subjective representations which signify nothing in the object.[54] He tells us that the judgment of aesthetic quality "does not depend upon any present concept of the object"[55] and that the aesthetic quality ascribed to the object is purely and inescapably subjective;[56] yet, despite all this, he teaches that the aesthetic judgment of taste "lays claim...to be valid for everyone."[57]

There is, to be sure, no explicit inconsistency between these diverse views since the aesthetic judgment is not cognitive. Yet the disparity between the assertion of the universal validity of the aesthetic judgment of feeling-without-concept and the denial of objective validity to the cognitive judgment of perception (of sensation-without-concept) calls for comment. For the extreme position ascribed to Kant by Kemp Smith and Lewis makes it not only impossible for

Kant to dream and to make judgments of perception, but also impossible for him to have aesthetic experience. I feel safe in saying that while Mr. Nahm might not care very much whether the sage of Königsberg could dream or not, he would vehemently reject any suspicion that Kant could not experience beauty.

I will concede that aesthetic judgments do not employ the dynamical categories and principles of substance, causality, and existence—at least I will not now discuss whether they do or not. But the mathematical categories and principles certainly do apply to the qualities we experience aesthetically. The concepts which Kant holds do *not* play a role in the construction of (pure) aesthetic experience are not categorial concepts but empirical. The quality of the object which is represented in aesthetic judgment "permits of being understood and reduced to concepts," he grants, "but in the aesthetic judgment it is not so reduced."[58] "The judgment of taste does not subsume under a concept at all."[59] How then can it be a judgment? This is comparable to the question asked in the previous section: How can a judgment of perception be a judgment at all?

The third *Critique* distinguishes two types of judgment or rather two ways of judging: the determinant and the reflective.

> If the universal (rule, principle, law [concept]) is given, the judgment
> which subsumes the particular under it is determinant.[60]

The categories are given, and the subsumption of particulars under them takes place by schematism.[61] The answer to the "difficulty" of §13 of the first *Critique* can be expressed in the new terminology as follows: the transcendental judgment by which experiences are categorized is determinant judgment. We do not have intuitions (inspectable intuitions) and look around, perhaps in vain, for categorial concepts which apply to them. This is an essential part of the Copernican Revolution with respect to categorial concepts.

"If, however," Kant continues, "only the particular is given and the universal has to be found for it, then the judgment is simply reflective."[62] There is no Copernican Revolution with respect to the concepts used in reflective judgments: "Reflection on the laws of nature adjusts itself to nature, and not nature to the conditions according to which we strive to obtain a concept of it."[63] The subsumability of the more specific concepts of nature (species) under more general concepts (genera) and of special laws under more general laws, and the harmony between what is given to our senses and our psychical apparatus for articulating and mastering it are *entirely contingent*, not a priori necessary. With respect to these reflective procedures of the mind, therefore, a "difficulty" like that of §13 of the first *Critique* recurs. The manifold of intuition and imagination might be so chaotic and variegated that no empirical concept could be found to apply to its parts; and even if that difficulty were not met with, the manifold of objective perceptions might be so various that no subsumptive arrangement of concepts could be fitted to it.[64] In the latter case, we might have the kind of experience Hegel contemptuously allowed Kant, viz., "a candlestick here and a snuff box there"; but we could not count on having K-experience, viz., nature as phenomena under law and specific laws as specifications of more general laws.

In the third *Critique*, therefore, Kant is impelled to give a "deduction" of the concept or rule of reflective judgment which will do for empirical concepts what the Deduction of the Categories in the first *Critique* did for a priori concepts of determinant judgment. The *Critique of Judgment* proceeds as if there were a Copernican Revolution with respect to empirical imagination and concepts by "prescrib[ing] a law, not to nature (as autonomy) but to itself (as heautonomy) to guide its reflection upon nature,"[65] "making it imperative upon us to proceed on the principle of the conformity of nature to our faculty of cognition."[66] Thus the teleological judgment of reflection is regulative: problematic with regard to the object, imperative with regard to the methodological procedure.

There is, then, a close analogy between the first *Critique* and the *Critique of Teleological Judgment*. This has been known from the beginning, since there is more than analogy; there is an actual overlap of teachings. What has not been recognized (to my knowledge, at least[67]) is the manner in which the *Critique of Aesthetic Judgment* seems to have grown out of the doctrines of the *Prolegomena* which were rejected in the second edition of the *Critique of Pure Reason*. In at least one crucial passage the vocabulary of the *Prolegomena* and *Critique of Aesthetic Judgment* is almost the same;[68] and almost everywhere there is some analogy between their arguments.

The problem of the *Critique of Aesthetic Judgment* is: How can a judgment which is like a judgment of perception in its independence of concepts and its reference exclusively to my own subjective experience of non-objectifiable representations nevertheless "resemble the logical judgment [= judgment of experience] in being presupposed valid for all men"?[69] A judgment of agreeableness is expressed in the Theaetetan mode to show its merely subjective validity: "Canary wine is agreeable to me"[70] is in this respect like a judgment of perception. But in judgments of taste, "One judges not merely for himself but for all men, and then speaks of beauty as if it were a property of things."[71] Judging without a concept,[72] one reaches a judgment of taste which is comparable in some respects to a judgment of experience which is got by "superadding" a categorial concept to a perception:

> judgment of agreeableness : judgment of taste =
> judgment of perception : judgment of experience.

Something, therefore, must be "superadded" to the judgment of agreeableness to make a judgment of taste. Like the category, it must be a priori if it is to give the judgment a claim to be valid for all men: but it cannot be a concept, for if it were it would convert the subjective judgment of "agreeableness to me" into a determinant cognitive judgment that everyone ought to agree to, namely that the Canary wine *is in fact agreeable to me*. What is needed, however, is some way of making the transition from "The music is agreeable to me" to "The music ought to be judged agreeable *by everyone*, that is to say, is beautiful."

What does this job, for Kant, is an a priori principle of the faculty of judgment, which refers disinterested pleasure to "that subjective factor which we may presuppose in all men (as requisite for a possible experience generally [= K-experience])" and which warrants us "in exacting from everyone the pleasure of the representation in respect of the relation of the cognitive faculties engaged in the estimate of a sensible object in general."[73] Instead of an intuitive image being subsumed under an empirical concept, as in a cognitive judgment of experience, the imagination *itself* is subsumed under the understanding as the *faculty* of concepts in general.

It is thus, I think, that the aesthetic experience, which is not cognitive, gets its place in consciousness under the transcendental unity of apperception. The aesthetic experience and the validity of aesthetic judgments, like illusions and dreams, are preserved without surreptitiously being converted into cognitive experiences and judgments.[75]

NOTES

1. *Mind and the World Order* (New York, 1929), p. 221. I discussed other aspects of Lewis's interpretation of Kant in "Lewis' Kantianism" in *Studies in the Philosophy of Kant* (Indianapolis: Bobbs-Merrill, 1965), pp. 108-24.

2. Ibid., p. 222. The entire sentence is italicized in the original.

3. *Critique of Pure Reason*, A 89-90 = B 122-23.

4. The quoted words are from H. J. de Vleeschauwer, *La déduction transcendentale dans l'oeuvre de Kant* (1936; New York, 1976), II, 176, who gives a survey of the divergent German-language interpretations.

5. Norman Kemp Smith, *A Commentary on Kant's Critique of Pure Reason* (London, 1923), p. 222.

6. H. J. Paton, *Kant's Metaphysic of Experience* (London, 1936), I, 324-25.

7. Lewis, *Mind and the World Order*, p. 221.

8. *Critique of Pure Reason*, B 1.

9. Ibid., A 19 = B 33.

10. Ibid., A 320 = B 377.

11. Ibid., A109; not in B. Kant often uses "appearances" where he means "representations," i.e., "appearances" often means "appearances to consciousness" and not "phenomena = objects."

12. This is pointed out by R. P. Wolff (*Kant's Theory of Mental Activity*, Harvard Univ. Press, 1963, p. 94), who does not, however, distinguish terminologically two meanings of "intuition." Philip Cummins, "Kant on Inner and Outer Intuition," *Nous* 2 (1968), 271-92, distinguishes between two ways in which the relation of intuition to its object may be conceived: the "intentional object" interpretation and the "objective constituent" interpretation. He holds that Kant did not clearly differentiate between them, and there is no suggestion that he moved from one to the other. What makes Cummins's essay relevant to our present concern, however, is that he tacitly indicates (p. 285) that the

problem of §13 arises for the *latter* interpretation, which resembles the view that intuition is "inspectable."

13. *Critique of Pure Reason*, A 104-05; not in B.

14. Ibid., A 191 = B 236.

15. Ibid., A 253 = B 309.

16. Ibid., A 247 = B 304.

17. Ibid., B 130.

18. Ibid., A 79; B 141.

19. Ibid., B 141. "Judgment is nothing but the manner in which given *Erkenntnisse* [intuitions and concepts] are brought to the objective unity of apperception."

20. Ibid., A 191 = B 236, cited and quoted in part above.

21. Ibid., A 108; not in B: "This transcendental unity of apperception forms out of all possible appearances, which can stand along side one another in one experience, a connection of all these representations according to laws.... The original and synthetic unity of the identity of the self is thus at the same time a consciousness of an equally necessary unity in the synthesis of all appearances according to concepts, that is, according to rules...which determine an object for their intuition, that is, the concept of something wherein they are necessarily interconnected."

22. Kemp Smith, *Commentary*, p. 222.

23. Paton, *Kant's Metaphysic of Experience*, I, 332 ff.

24. Reflexion 6315 (Ak. XVIII, 621), italics added. Kant is discussing specifically the imagination "in dreams or in fever." The imaginations in these cases are called *Sinnesanschauungen* but "only in the imagination, to which the object outside the representation is not present." That is, imagination may produce intuitions in the inspectional but not in the functional sense.

25. *Critique of Pure Reason*, A 112; similarly A 111, line 33; neither in B.

26. Ibid., A 120; not in B.

27. Ibid.

28. Ibid., A 112; not in B.

29. Letter to Marcus Herz, May 26, 1789 (Ak. XI, 52; Zweig, *Kant's Philosophical Correspondence*, p. 153).

30. In the next two sections of this paper we shall take up this claim.

31. *Critique of Pure Reason*, B §18; cf. B xl-xli. See P. F. Strawson, *The Bounds of Sense*, pp. 92, 101, 109. Even closer to the point I am about to make is Eva Schaper, "Kant on Imagination," *The Philosophical Forum* 2 (1971), 430-45: "Imagination must ...be parasitic upon experience of a real, non-imagined world" (p. 445).

32. *Prolegomena*, §13, Remark III (Ak. IV, 290).

33. *Critique of Pure Reason*, B 278.

34. Ibid., A 99-100; B 140.

35. *Prolegomena*, §20 (Ak. IV, 300, line 8; Beck translation, p. 48, line 5). This content of inner experience (L-experience) is called "empirical self-knowledge" and is identified with the subject of empirical psychology (Reflexion 5453). Yet to be even knowledge of the self (expressible in judgments) it must be *categorized* without being *objectified* in the normal sense (viz., ascribed by outer sense to a spatial object); see p. 53 below.

36. The problem which is worrying us here must have been brought to Kant's attention by Kiesewetter, who had many extensive conversations with Kant in 1788-89 and again in 1791. It was Kant's practice then to write brief essays in answer to Kiesewetter's

questions. One is entitled: "Beantwortung der Frage: Ist es eine Erfahrung, daß wir denken?", Reflexion 5661 (Ak. XVIII, 318-20).

Kant defines *Erfahrung* as "the judgment that expresses an empirical cognition" and asserts that we think something is not, *an sich*, an experience. "Gleichwohl aber bringt dieser Gedanke einen Gegenstand der Erfahrung hervor oder eine Bestimmung des Gemüths, die beobachtet werden kann, sofern es nämlich durch das Denkungsvermögen afficiert wird." My knowledge of that which this thought is *about* is *Erfahrung* but it makes no reference to the time when the thought occurred, whereas the consciousness of the thought (sc. the act of thinking) does so. Kant then quickly develops an infinite regress on the assumption that the awareness of my thought is itself an experience (i.e., has a determinate place in objective time); the objective time under which ("unter der," not "in der") the thinking took place would in turn have to be constituted by an act of mind, "welches ungereimt ist." Hence: "Das Bewußtsein aber, eine Erfahrung anzustellen oder auch überhaupt zu denken, ist ein *transzendentales Bewußtsein, nicht Erfahrung*" (p. 319). In another essay for Kiesewetter (Reflexion 6311, Ak. XVIII, 610), "transcendental consciousness" means merely "the consciousness, I think." (The term "transcendental consciousness" does not occur in the first *Critique*.)

37. Kemp Smith, *Commentary*, pp. 288-89; Paton, *Kant's Metaphysic of Experience*, I, 330-31. Only Gerold Prauss (*Erscheinung bei Kant*, [Berlin, 1971], pp. 139-254) and G. Buchdahl (*Metaphysics and the Philosophy of Science* [Oxford, 1969], p. 636 and passim) have made serious efforts to salvage the *Prolegomena* teaching. Both de Vleeschauwer (*La déduction transcendentale*, II, 490) and Graham Bird (*Kant's Theory of Knowledge* [London, 1962], pp. 115-16) have given unusually sympathetic accounts of Kant's reasons for holding the *Prolegomena* doctrine.

38. Even the genetic psychology of the first paragraph of B is repeated in *Prol.* §18, where Kant says all our judgments are "at first merely judgments of perception...and we do not until afterward give them a new reference to an object."

39. *Prolegomena*, §18 (Ak. IV, 298, line 3; Beck p. 45, bottom).

40. Ibid., §19 and note.

41. *Critique of Pure Reason*, B 141.

42. Ibid., B 141-42.

43. *Prolegomena*, §20, para. 1.

44. Kant's example is merely "When the sun shines on the stone it becomes warm." But the sense he must want requires the judgment to be in the autobiographical or even Theaetetan mode, as in Reflexion 3145 (Ak. XVI (2), 678). Accordingly, in the part of the *Critique of Pure Reason* which comes closest to repeating the *Prolegomena* distinction, Kant contrasts, "if I support a body, I feel an impression of weight" with "it, the body, is heavy" (B 142).

45. *Critique of Pure Reason*, A 189 = B 234; cf. A 108, end. The point is well made by Max Apel, *Kommentar zu Kants Prolegomena* (2d ed., 1923), p. 160, and by R. P. Wolff, *Kant's Theory of Mental Activity*, p. 280.

46. *Critique of Pure Reason*, A 166 = B 208. This was pointed out (so far as I know for the first time) by Prauss (*Erscheinung bei Kant*, p. 163). He states (p. 143) that Kant nowhere speaks of judgments of perception that do not *enthalten* a category. Although I have learned much from this book I disagree with him here. (I do not here discuss the question as to whether *any* judgment can *enthalten* a category unless the name of the category is mentioned. My view is in deeper disagreement with what he means.) Kant clearly says that judgments of perception "bedürfen keines reinen Verstandesbegriffs"

(*Prol*, §18, Ak. IV, 298, lines 3-4). Prauss writes: "Es [ist] auch niemals einfach 'die Kategorie', was Kant den Wahrnehmungsurteilen jeweils abspricht, sondern ebenfalls allein diese *Anwendung* der Kategorie" (p. 162) where "diese Anwendung" means "Deutung von Erscheinungen" presumably in the manner of schematism (see p. 104). This, I argue, is true, but it is not supported by Kant's words cited above.

47. *Prolegomena*, §19 note.

48. Kant seems to have had unusual difficulty in making up his mind, or at least in expressing his ideas, on secondary qualities. In *Vorlesung über Logik*, §40 note, "The stone is warm" is called a judgment of experience; in *Prolegomena*, §19, "The room is warm" is called a judgment of perception! In the *Critique of Pure Reason* he holds that colors "are not properties of the bodies to the intuition of which they are attached." Yet in *Logik*, §40 note, "This tower is red" is "a judgment of experience, i.e., an empirical judgment through which I get a concept of the object." In direct contradiction to the statement quoted in the first sentence of this section, the *Critique of Judgment*, §1, says, "Every reference of representations is capable of being objective, even that of sensations (in which case it signifies the real in an empirical representation)." The view I have constructed in the body of the paper seems to me to be sound and perhaps captures a large part of what Kant meant; it conforms most closely to the views expressed in the *Critique of Judgment*, Introduction VII.

49. Prauss, *Erscheinung bei Kant*, pp. 120, 215-16, 137, 145.

50. Lewis, *Mind and the World Order*, p. 225.

51. The representations which may not be accompanied by consciousness (*Critique of Pure Reason*, A 320 = B 376) are like Leibniz's *petites perceptions*. If there were not the understanding, I would not be able to *know* I have even sense data; "consequently for me, *as a knowing being*, they would be absolutely nothing. They could still (*I imagine myself to be an animal*) carry on their play in an orderly fashion, as representations connected according to the empirical laws of association, and thus even have an influence on my feeling and desire, without my being aware of them (assuming even that I am conscious of each individual representation but not of their relation to the unity of representation of their object by means of the synthetic unity of their apperception). This might be so without my knowing the slightest thing thereby, not even what my own condition is." Letter to Marcus Herz, May 26, 1789 (Ak. XI, 52; Zweig, *Correspondence*, pp. 153-54), italics added.

52. Milton C. Nahm, *Aesthetic Experience and its Presuppositions*, p. 119.

53. *Prolegomena*, §18, end.

54. For instance, *First Introduction to the Critique of Judgment* (Haden translation), p. 28. *Critique of Judgment*, Ak. V, 189 (Meredith, p. 29). On this, unlike secondary qualities, Kant is uniformly consistent.

55. *Critique of Judgment*, Introduction VII, Ak. V, 190 (Meredith, p. 31).

56. Ibid., Ak. V, 189 (Meredith, p. 29).

57. Ibid., Introduction VII, Ak. V, 191 (Meredith, p. 91).

58. Ibid., "General Remark on the Exposition of Aesthetic Reflective Judgments," Ak. V, 266 (Meredith, p. 117).

59. Ibid., §35, Ak. V, 286 (Meredith, p. 142).

60. Ibid., Introduction IV, Ak. V, 179 (Meredith, p. 18).

61. Ibid., Introduction V, Ak. V, 183 (Meredith, p. 22). See *Critique of Pure Reason*, A 138 = B 177.

62. *Critique of Judgment*, Introduction IV, Ak. V, 179 (Meredith, p. 18).

63. Ibid., Ak. V, 180 (Meredith, p. 19).

64. *First Introduction to the Critique of Judgment* (Haden translation), p. 14.

65. *Critique of Judgment*, Introduction V, Ak. V, 185 (Meredith, p. 25).

66. Ibid., Introduction VI, Ak. V., 188 (Meredith, pp. 28-29).

67. The analogy between the two types of judgment in the third *Critique* and in the *Prolegomena* has been noticed by Walter Cerf in his introduction to his translation of the "Analytic of the Beautiful" (Bobbs-Merrill, 1963), p. xxxiv; T. E. Uehling, *The Notion of Form in Kant's Critique of Judgment* (Mouton, 1971), p. 52; and Donald Crawford, *Kant's Aesthetic Theory* (University of Wisconsin Press, 1974), p. 34; but they did not exploit the resemblance in the way I here attempt to do.

68. *Critique of Judgment*, §13, talks about *Erfahrungsurteile* (using this word which occurs only three times in the *Critique of Pure Reason*, at B 12 and 13, in passages which are taken verbatim from the *Prolegomena*, and at B 41 where it is simply a synonym for "empirical judgment" in contrast to a judgment of geometry known a priori). I do not find *Wahrnehmungsurteile* in either the first or the third *Critiques*, but in §36 of the *Critique of Judgment* Kant uses *Empfindungsurteil* as a synonym for *Wahrnehmungsurteil*. More usually *logisches Urteil* is used in the *Critique of Judgment*.

69. *Critique of Judgment*, §6, Ak. V, 211 (Meredith, p. 51).

70. Ibid., §7, Ak. V, 212 (Meredith, p. 51).

7 1. Ibid., §7, Ak. V, 212 (Meredith, p. 52).

72. Ibid., §35, Ak. V, 286 (Meredith, p. 142).

73. Ibid., §38, Ak. V, 290 (Meredith, p. 147). Notice also how the objective validity of the judgment of taste depends upon the *Gemeinsinn* (*Critique of Judgment*, §20) just as the objective validity of the judgment of experience depends upon its status for *Bewußtsein überhaupt* (*Prolegomena*, §§20, 22).

74. *Critique of Judgment*, §35, Ak. V, 287 (Meredith, p. 143).

75. [This essay originally appeared in *Akten des IV. internationalen Kant-Kongresses* (Berlin: De Gruyter,1975), Part III, pp. 26-43, and is reprinted with permission.]

Analytic and Synthetic Judgments before Kant

> Men who never think independently have nevertheless the acuteness
> to discover everything, after it has been once shown them, in what
> was said long since, though no one was ever able to see it there be-
> fore.
>
> Prolegomena, §3
>
> Es ist auch schon das gewöhnliche Schicksal alles Neuen in Wissen-
> schaften, wenn man ihm nichts entgegensetzen kann, daß man es
> doch wenigstens als längst bekannt bei Älteren antreffe.
>
> Über eine Entdeckung nach der alle neue Kritik
der reinen Vernunft durch eine ältere entbehrlich
gemacht werden soll (Ak. VIII, 242).

It is perhaps customary in introductory courses in the history of philosophy, and it is not unknown in the literature—including some of my own writings—to introduce Kant's distinction between analytic and synthetic judgments by referring to Leibniz's distinction between truths of reason and truths of fact and to Hume's distinction between relations of ideas and matters of fact. Some, more venturesome perhaps, seek the origin of the distinction in Locke's dichotomy of trifling and instructive propositions, in Hobbes's of truths of universal propositions and truths of existential propositions, and even farther back in truths dependent upon the intellect of God and those dependent upon the will of God.

Under the common assumption that pre-Kantian philosophers equated whatever in their terminology is said to be equivalent to "analytic" with a priori and whatever in their terminology is said to be equivalent to "synthetic" with a posteriori, the following summary table is not uncommon:

	a priori	*a posteriori*
analytic	relations of ideas truths of reason	none
synthetic	none	matters of fact truths of fact

The schema just presented is not exactly wrong, but it is woefully incomplete. It was the thesis of a famous paper by Arthur O. Lovejoy[1] that the table was so incomplete and wrong that it created the fiction that Kant had something original to contribute besides a new terminology, and that if the contribution of one other philosopher (Wolff) is put into the table, it will turn out that Kant was either a mere plagiarist or else unpardonably ignorant of the state of the problem.

Indeed one of the most remarkable things, which ought first to strike the eye, is that Kant *seems to have been ignorant of the information summarized in the table.* For he says, "Perhaps even the distinction between analytic and synthetic judgments has never previously been considered,"[2] and, more specifically, "the dogmatic philosophers Wolff and his acute follower Baumgarten altogether neglected this apparently obvious distinction."[3]

Yet in the same paragraph in the *Prolegomena* he says he finds "an indication of the division" in Locke's *Essay,* Book IV, chapter 3, §§9-10, where Locke draws a distinction between our certainty of identity and diversity (Kant says "identity or contradiction"—a significant slip) and that of coexistence, of which we have little a priori knowledge. But he seems to have overlooked a more obvious source, namely, Book IV, chapters 7 and 8, of the *Essay,* where Locke distinguishes between "a real truth [which] conveys with it instructive real knowledge" by stating "a necessary consequence of a precise complex idea...not contained in it," and "trifling propositions" which are either mere identities or affirmations "when any part of a complex idea is predicated of the whole."[4] Thus it seems that Locke had not only distinguished between analytic and synthetic judgments but that he had held, and that Kant knew that he had held, that some of the latter could be known with certainty, that is, that they were a priori.

In the same paragraph, Kant says that Locke was so vague and indefinite in his remarks on a priori synthetic knowledge that he did not stimulate even Hume "to make investigations concerning this sort of propositions." Yet again and again Kant writes as if Hume had distinguished between analytic and synthetic judgments and had categorically denied the possibility of a priori synthetic judgments. He did so, Kant held, because he failed to draw a needed distinction between the synthetic judgments of the understanding, which may be known a priori for objects of possible experience, and those of reason, which profess to be about things which can never be met with in experience. Since Hume agreed with Kant that the latter type of synthetic a priori knowledge is impossible, his failure to make the needed distinction led him to reject the possibility of any synthetic judgments (of possible experience) known a priori, while Kant, precisely by making this distinction, did not have to condemn all a priori synthetic judgments but only those which claim to refer beyond experience.[5]

Hence Hume concluded, according to Kant, that all *genuine* a priori knowledge must be analytic. Concerning the judgments which are commonly believed to be a priori but not analytic (such as the causal maxim), Hume went on to give a psychological explanation of the illusion that they are a priori. Since Kant had such insights into Hume's mode of argument, I cannot explain why he did not cite the opening paragraphs of Section IV of the *Enquiry*, a passage known to every schoolboy. Here Hume draws his famous distinction between relations of ideas and matters of fact. Kant must have read there: "The contrary of every matter of fact is still possible because it can never imply a contradiction and is conceived by the mind with the same facility and distinctness as if ever so conformable to reality." In the *Enquiry*, therefore, matter of fact judgments meet one of the criteria of syntheticity. Accordingly, relations of ideas "discoverable by the mere operation of thought without dependence on what is anywhere existent in the universe" seem to be judged in what Kant called analytic judgments.

Yet had Kant read the *Treatise* he would have discovered that perhaps Hume did not mean exactly what he seemed to be saying; and if we, who can read the *Treatise*, do so, we perhaps can find out why Kant was correct in not taking this to mean that relations of ideas, even if (presumably) testable by contradiction, are equivalent to the relation expressed in an analytical judgment. The relations of ideas in the *Enquiry* correspond to the "necessary and unalterable" philosophical relations of the *Treatise*, relations "which depend entirely on the ideas which we compare together."[6] But the necessary and unalterable philosophical relations are not analytical in the sense that one of the relata is included in the other, nor in the sense that the denial of such a relation involves a formal contradiction.[7]

By "contradiction" Hume did not mean merely an assertion like "A is not A." He means also "A is not B" where an A that is not a B is "inconceivable" or "unimaginable."

> Wherein consists the difference betwixt believing and disbelieving any proposition? The answer is easy with regard to propositions, that are prov'd by intuition or demonstration. In that case, the person, who assents, not only conceives the ideas according to the proposition, but is necessarily determin'd to conceive them in that particular manner, either immediately or by the imposition of other ideas. Whatever is absurd is unintelligible; nor is it possible for the imagination to conceive anything contrary to a demonstration.[8]

Thus even before Kant there were ambiguities which have recently been brought to light again in the continuing debate about the criterion of analyticity, though of course Hume is more ambiguous than those whom Quine is criticizing. For Hume did not mean by "contradiction" a formal contradiction alone; "inconceivability" means not merely logical nonsense, but also unimaginability, and even counter-intuitivity. His relations of ideas are not trifling propositions nor are they analytical propositions as Kant understood the term, though this cannot be seen by anyone who, like Kant, reads only the *Enquiry* and not also the *Treatise*. Had Kant read Hume's *Treatise,* he would have found Hume tacitly admitting a class of intuitively and demonstratively necessary relations of ideas which are not testable by the logical law of contradiction.

Hume differed from Locke in holding that the causal relation is neither intuitively nor demonstratively known. Hence he concluded that it is a matter-of-fact relation which can be known, if at all, only a posteriori. It was this inference which awoke Kant from his dogmatic slumber. He "generalized Hume's problem" and saw that if the syntheticity of the causal maxim implied its aposteriority, then all the propositions even of mathematics (as well as metaphysics) can be known only a posteriori. He held that Hume himself had been saved from the absurdity of holding mathematics to be a posteriori only because he had made the mistake of holding its judgments to be analytic.[9] Believing as Kant did that mathematical judgments were both synthetic and a priori, he had to investigate how it is possible for there to be such judgments, and he "solemnly and legally suspended" all metaphysicians from their occupation until they had answered the question of how this was possible.[10]

Leibniz's distinction between truths of reason and truths of fact is another obvious source of Kant's distinction which he does not anywhere mention. Its *locus classicus* is the *Monadology*:

> 31. Our reasonings are grounded on two great principles, that of contradiction, in virtue of which we judge false that which involves a contradiction, and true that which is opposed or contradictory to the false.

> 33. There are also two kinds of truths, those of reason and those of fact. Truths of reason are necessary and their opposite is impossible. When a truth is necessary, its reason can be found by analysis, resolving it into more simple ideas and truths, until we come to those that are primary.

> 35. There are simple ideas, of which no definition can be given; there are also axioms and postulates, in a word, primary principles; and these are identical propositions whose opposite involves an express contradiction.

From these well-known passages it is inferred that truths of fact are synthetic and truths of reason are analytic, and that only the latter can be known a priori. But we must remember that the *Monadology* was a book for popular consumption, and the esoteric doctrine of Leibniz, which we know mostly through his unpublished writings, is very much more complicated.

According to the esoteric doctrine, in all true affirmative propositions the concept of the predicate is included in the concept of the subject.[11] Therefore all true affirmative propositions are identities or partial identities (that is, analytic propositions), and all false affirmative propositions are self-contradictory. If the demonstration of the proposition by reduction to an identity through substitution of definientia for definienda can be accomplished in a finite number of steps, the judgment is called an explicit identity even though its form is not "A is A" but rather "A.B is B" or "A is A.B." If the reduction cannot be effected in a finite number of steps, the proposition is only a virtual identity and cannot be known by showing the self-contradictoriness of its contradictory; though intrinsically analytic, it is known to us in other ways than an expressly analytic judgment.[12]

The *Monadology* gives a succinct account of how we know a theorem in geometry, without taking these esoteric complications into account: by substituting definientia we come to axioms, and axioms are explicit identities whose "opposites involve an express contradiction." Earlier (1678) in a letter to Conring Leibniz had written:

> Demonstration is a chain of definitions.... All truths can be resolved
> into definitions, identical propositions, and observations though
> purely intelligible truths do not need observations. [13]

But there are two places where this program breaks down, at least one of which Leibniz himself admitted.

1. There must be *primae veritates* which are unprovable and therefore not analytic, because explicit identity or contradiction cannot obtain between simple unanalyzable terms. The contradictory of a *prima veritas* cannot, in spite of §35 of the *Monadology*, be self-contradictory. In Russell's words: "Any relation between simple ideas is necessarily synthetic. For the analytic relation...can only hold between ideas of which one at least is complex."[14]

In a work unknown to his contemporaries but known to Kant, Leibniz seems to have seen this difficulty. He substituted "comparison or concurrence (*concours*)" for the stricter "identity and contradiction" between simple ideas.[15] He furthermore distinguished primitive truths known by intuition into two kinds: primitive truths of reason and primitive truths of fact.

Under primitive truths of reason he listed "identical affirmatives," which are trifling, and "identical negatives," which are either under the law of contradiction or are "disparates." "Disparates" are propositions that state that the object of one idea is not the object of another idea, as "that heat is not the same thing as color." Disparates "may be asserted independently of all proof or of reduction to opposition or to the principle of contradiction."[16]

2. A like problem is met with not merely at the end of a reduction to identity, but along the course of the reduction from an apparently synthetic judgment to an identity. Definition must be reached by analyzing complex concepts and then demonstrating the identity of the analysantia. In order to give real definitions (merely nominal definitions trivialize the project[17]), we must be able to show the compossibility and necessary coherence of predicates in a complex concept. If these predicates are simple (conceived per se) it cannot be demonstrated that they must co-inhere in one subject concept by appealing to the law of contradiction, because there is no formal contradiction in the conjunction of two simple predicates.

As Russell says, "This compatibility, since it is presupposed by the analytic judgment, cannot itself be analytic";[18] and Leibniz himself says:

> As often as I combine several things which are not conceived through
> themselves, experience is needed, not only of the fact that they are

conceived by me at the same time in the same subject...but also of the
fact that they really exist in the same subject.[19]

(Perhaps by "experience" Leibniz here means to include intuition and not
merely empirical observation, which he excluded in his letter to Conring cited
above.)

From all this it follows that while Leibniz had, in his *exoteric* works, a rea-
sonably clear distinction between analytic and synthetic judgments, he was not
able to maintain in his *esoteric* works that all a priori judgments are analytic. It
may well be that Kant was thinking of Leibniz when he wrote:

> As it was found that the conclusions of mathematicians all proceed
> according to the law of contradiction...men persuaded themselves that
> the fundamental principles were known by the same law. This was a
> great mistake, for a synthetical proposition can indeed be established
> by the law of contradiction but only by presupposing another
> synthetical proposition from which it follows, but never by that law
> alone.[20]

Wolff had an easier task than Leibniz because he did not adhere to Leibniz's
analytical theory of judgment according to which *praedicatum inest subiecto*.[21]
For him, judgment is the *Verknüpfung* or *Trennung* (connection or separation) of
two concepts.[22] With this definition he inquired into the ground of the connection or separation of the concepts and found it in the subject as the *Bedingung* of
the predicate (*Aussage*) according to the principle of sufficient reason. But the
latter principle was for him a logical principle, demonstrable by the law of contradiction; and hence Wolff did not adequately distinguish between the way in
which a subject implies a predicate in what we call an analytical proposition and
the way in which it is a mere condition in what we call a synthetic judgment.[23]
Thus he did not emphasize the difference between identities and other necessary
propositions connecting simple ideas, which ought to have kept him from holding that the denials of the latter are self-contradictory as are the denials of the
former.[24] He recognizes that the connection of two simple ideas is not "thought
through identity" because they do not determine one another, but "*fieri posse
constat (sive vi experientiae, sive demonstrationis) combinari posse intelliguntur*"[25] and this *combinari posse* can be seen by *ratio intuitiva*. A concept is
gedenkbar if one can see the agreement (*consensio, convenientia*) of the components. But he falls back into the old way of thinking when he holds that the
ungedenkbare combinations are self-contradictory.[26] This is certainly how Kant
read him: "The only conflict they (the Leibniz-Wolffians) recognize is that of
contradiction."[27] Because he placed so much more emphasis on the
self-contradictoriness of the contradictory than on the intuition of the *consensio*,
he was vulnerable to attack from men like Crusius, as we shall see.

We turn now to Wolff's theory of the constitution of complex subjects (*notiones foecundae*[28]). With such a subject, the criterion of the self-contradictoriness of the contradictory of a judgment is more apt. For now he is considering truly analytical judgments; but the whole burden of proof is shifted from synthetic *judgments* to synthetic *subjects*. Lambert criticized him for this, saying that he took nominal definitions "as it were gratis" and "without noticing it, hid all the difficulties in them."[29] This, however, is unfair to Wolff, for he devoted much effort to establishing the real possibility (not merely the logical possibility) of complex concepts.[30] Regrettably, however, Wolff (perhaps not clearly seeing the importance of the distinction) does not give in any systematic order the criteria by which the real possibility of a concept is to be decided, that is, by which the possibility of the co-inherence of independent *essentialia*[31] is to be established. But he does, in various places in the *Ontologia*, provide several conditions. One—"*ab existentia ad possibilitatem valet consequentia*"[32]—is a posteriori, four (or five) others are apparently a priori. A concept consisting of the *notae* A and B is a priori possible if A and B presuppose one another or if one follows from the other by demonstration.[33] (For these, presumably, the law of contradiction suffices.) Another test is the constructability of the concept.[34] This is, at least verbally, an anticipation of the test for the possibility of mathematical concepts in Kant. But Wolff does not expand on this and probably did not see the significance of what he had said, since he regarded the syllogism, not construction, as the paradigm of mathematical proof.[35] Finally there is the "*combinari posse intelliguntur*" to which I have already alluded. The last, and perhaps the next to last, are the only ones which can build synthetic real concepts a priori. The ones about demonstrability are obviously inadequate for the addition of independent predicates, and the first one does so only a posteriori.

In summary, then, Wolff admits two kinds of propositions whose contradictories he holds to be self-contradictory:

1. Empty sentences, *propositio identica* ("A is A"), sometimes[36] called axioms.

2. Judgments *per essentialia, modus praedicandi essentialia*[37] ("A is B" where A is a complex concept in which B is an *essentia*), elsewhere called axioms[38] and identities.[39]

Lovejoy[40] calls (2) synthetical judgments a priori because they have a synthetical or "fecund" subject, but they are clearly analytical by Kant's criterion.

To these must be added a third type of judgment, some of which can be known a priori and others a posteriori:

3. Judgments *per attributum, modus praedicandi attributa*[41] ("A is C" where C is an attribute of A not included in its definition or essence but having its sufficient reason in the essence).

Since it is judgments of this kind that were claimed later, by Eberhard, to be synthetic and known a priori, we might wish that Wolff had given a systematic treatment of them in some one place. His examples, however, are instructive.

a. His first example is meant to be a judgment known a priori: "It is an attribute of a triangle (*Dreyeck*) that it has three angles (*Winkel*). For this is attributed to it (*kommet ihm zu*) because a triangle is a space enclosed in three lines."[42] Presumably this is a logical "because," since the proposition is supposed to be reducible to axioms and definitions which are identities;[43] but elsewhere he says it is evident "by construction."[44]

b. "Hardness is an attribute of stone but not of wax" is obviously a posteriori, and Wolff tells us how to find out by experience which predicates are attributes and which are mere accidents of things.[45]

c. Finally, there are judgments which can be known a priori in the sense that, as Kant says, they cannot "be derived immediately from experience but from a universal rule"; but they are not a priori ("completely a priori," as Kant says) in the sense that they can be known completely independently of all experience, since the "universal rule" is itself based upon experience.[46] Wolff holds that one can "prove" a judgment *per attributum* by syllogism. His example is "Wood can be cut."[47] The proof is given by providing a definition of cutting ("the separation of parts") and of wood ("Made up of fibers"). Such a proof converts "historical" (that is, empirical) knowledge into "philosophical" knowledge or "knowledge of the reason of things."[48]

Crusius, the principal pre-Kantian critic of Wolff, is now largely forgotten, but Kant himself did not forget him. Long before Hume awoke Kant from his dogmatic slumber, Crusius[49] had already pointed out what Kant was later to relearn from Hume at a critical point in his own development when the impact of Hume's discovery about causality "gave quite a new direction to [Kant's] investigations."[50]

J. S. Beck[51] in 1793 wrote Kant that Crusius's *Weg zur Gewißheit* (1747) provided a better "indication" of the analytic-synthetic distinction than the passages Kant had cited from Locke, but Kant knew Crusius's work already in the 1760s. In his *Dissertatio de use et limitibus principii rationis determinantis, vulgo sufficientis* (1743) Crusius had criticized Wolff's attempted derivation[52] of the principle of sufficient reason from the principle of contradiction. In his *Entwurf der nothwendigen Vernunftwahrheiten* (1745) and *Weg zur Gewißheit* he had criticized Wolff for believing in the sufficiency of the principle of contradiction for the establishment and testing of a priori truth. "The question," he says, "is not whether, upon presupposing [certain] concepts we are required by the law of contradiction to deny the opposite; this is well known. The question is: whether the law of contradiction was, or even could have been, the sufficient reason for the constitution (*Einrichtung*) of the concepts themselves."[53] He answers this question in the negative.

He takes the case of causality.[54] "Every effect has a cause" is clear from the principle of contradiction, but that does not show that the existence of one thing is dependent on that of another. The latter can be denied without contradiction, because the subjects to which existence is attributed are different and exist at different times. Experience, even Wolff saw, must be called upon to discover what *specific* thing is the cause of another; but, unlike Wolff, Crusius believed that the general principle cannot be established merely by a proof from the law of contradiction. That is to say, in Kantian language, Crusius sought a proof of the principle of causality as, or as derived from, a synthetic a priori principle. Real knowledge must be founded on a different principle from the law of contradiction, which suffices for what Crusius calls "hypothetical knowledge."

We have seen earlier philosophers supplement demonstration with intuition so as to have two bases for certain knowledge. Hume denied that the causal principle is known in either way, and therefore asserted that it is not known a priori. Crusius, on the contrary, supplements demonstrative knowledge with two *Vernunftwahrheiten* (truths of reason) which he calls the "principles of inseparability and uncombinability": "Whatever two things cannot be thought apart from one another cannot exist or be possible apart from one another," and "Whatever two things cannot be thought with and beside one another cannot be possible or exist with and beside one another."[55] These give the ground why contradictories cannot coexist or be compossible, but they go far beyond the realm of the merely logically impossible. The real ground of a predicate or a relation must be distinguished from the logical ground, and the connection of real ground with the predicate can by known a priori; but the real ground itself can be known only through experience.

Not only did Crusius have a clear conception of the difference between analytic and synthetic judgments; he also had a theory as to how synthetic judgments are possible a priori. It was not a theory that Kant could accept, as he accepted the consequences of Crusius's distinction between judgments from logical grounds and judgments from real grounds. After a long period in which he honored Crusius for drawing the right distinction he turned against him for failing to show how synthetic judgments can be known a priori: Crusius, he said, made mere custom and incapacity to think otherwise into an objective necessity, and could get to objective necessity only by accepting a preestablished harmony between innate ideas and their objects.[56] But what Kant did learn from Crusius must not be underestimated; he learned that "the rain never follows the wind because of the law of identity."[57]

I shall not attempt to recount the steps by which Kant was led to make his classical distinction between synthetic and analytic judgments. I refrain from this for two reasons: first, we do not actually know what they were or when they were taken; and second, what is known about them has already been adequately presented.[58] Rather than going through this history of the development of the distinction, I wish rather to turn to a defense of the originality of his distinction which Kant made late in his life: *On a Discovery according to which the Whole New Critique of Pure Reason is Rendered Unnecessary by an Earlier One*, published in 1790 against Eberhard.[59] This is an important paper both historically and philosophically—historically because it is Kant's *Auseinandersetzung* with the Wolffian tradition; philosophically, because it shows us how Kant would answer his modern critics who deny that there are synthetic judgments known a priori—for most modern critics have, perhaps unbeknownst to themselves, merely repeated Eberhard's criticisms.[60]

On p. 109 above, I gave Wolff's division of judgments which are not formal identities into judgments *per essentialia* and judgments *per attributum*. Eberhard holds that they are both a priori, and that whatever is valid in Kant's distinction between analytic and synthetic judgments a priori coincides with Wolff's distinction. Eberhard calls judgments *per attributum* synthetic because they affirm attributes which are not included in the essence of the subject concept, and a priori because they have their sufficient ground in the subject concept from which they may be explicated by analysis. Hence Eberhard holds that the problem to which the *Critique of Pure Reason* is addressed—namely, "How are synthetic judgments a priori possible?"—had already been answered by Wolff, and that all Kant contributed was a new (and confusing) terminology. Against the accusation that the distinction was already known and was not invented by Kant, Kant replied:

> Maybe so! But the reason why the importance of the distinction has not been recognized seems to be that all a priori judgments were regarded [by Wolff] as analytic...so the whole point of the distinction disappeared.[61]

In modern terminology (which we owe to C. I. Lewis)[62] "synthetic judgments a priori" are sometimes said to be implicitly analytic judgments—ampliative ("synthetic") by the criterion of "what is actually thought in the subject concept, though not so distinctly and with the same (full) consciousness,"[63] but explicative ("analytic") by the criterion of logical deducibility and testability by the law of contradiction.

Kant and Eberhard agree—Kant accusingly, Eberhard proudly[64]—that the distinction between essence and attribute which underlies Eberhard's analytic-synthetic distinction is one drawn in general logic. But, Kant says, "The explanation of the possibility of synthetic judgments is a problem with which general logic has nothing to do. It need not even so much as know the problem by name."[65] In short, the problem as Kant sees it is one of epistemology, or what he calls transcendental logic; hence he feels justified in classifying judgments according to their *grounds (Wahrheitsgründe)*[66] and not merely as they are classified in formal logic (*per essentialia, per attributum*).

The essence with which Eberhard is concerned consists of those marks (*notae*) that are the necessary and sufficient conditions for the definition of the concept. The attributes for Eberhard are those marks that logically follow from the concept of the subject ("belong to it") but are not explicitly included in the logical essence or its definiens ("do not lie in it").[67] We can be sure that a predicate signifies an attribute if it is a logical consequence of the essence or definition, so that its denial would be self-contradictory. Thus "having more than two sides" is an attribute of a triangle, since "having three sides," the essence of triangle, logically entails "having more than two sides." An attribute which follows analytically from the definition or logical essence by the law of contradiction, as this one does, is called by Kant an "analytical predicate." Even though the judgment containing such a predicate may be ampliative or instructive for someone who does not know the implications of the definition, Kant is now content to call a judgment analytical if it contains an analytical predicate.[68]

But Kant holds that there is another kind of essence which he calls "real" instead of "logical," and another kind of attribute,[69] which he calls "synthetic" instead of "analytic."

A synthetic attribute, a *Bestimmung*,[70] is one which does not follow from the logical essence and yet has a sufficient ground in the real essence.[71] Hence it can be necessarily predicated of the subject in a synthetic judgment. Such a judgment is a priori synthetic. (To cite Kant's own example, that space has three dimensions is not known by analysis of the definition of space [its logical essence] and yet can be known a priori to be true of space.)

The problem of the *Critique of Pure Reason* is to see how an attribute can be attached synthetically, yet a priori, to an object whose concept does not logically entail it by containing it implicitly.

A concept is logically possible if it does not entail contradictory predicates. But a logically possible concept may be without an object and thus only an *ens rationis*.[72] To be shown to be really and not merely logically possible, the concept must be of an object which "agrees with the formal conditions of experience"[73] (First Postulate of Empirical Thought), and this includes the condition of sensible intuitability.

If the sensible intuition is empirical, that is, a real perception, the concept of the perceived object is really possible because whatever is actual is possible. A judgment founded on a perception is synthetic, but a posteriori.

Sensible intuition, whether pure or empirical, cannot reveal the ontologically real essence of a thing, which is even more hidden from Kant than it was from Locke. But if the sensible intuition is pure, it reveals the real essence[74] of the thing since it is an intuition of the condition under which alone a thing can be an object for us. Though Kant calls it the real essence, to avoid confusion between what, for Kant, is known a priori and what, for him and Locke, is not known at all, let us call it the *phenomenal essence*. It consists of all the conditions of an object that are necessary if it is possible for us to experience it.

What follows from the phenomenal essence is a synthetic attribute because it is not contained in, or found by the analysis of, the logical essence. The synthetic attribute follows from the sole condition under which the object can be known, not from its metaphysical (supersensible) real essence. By virtue of the necessity with which the synthetic attribute follows from the phenomenal essence, the judgment containing this attribute is known a priori. Because it does not follow by the law of contradiction from the logical essence, it is synthetic. Hence a judgment whose predicate signifies an attribute of the phenomenal essence is a synthetic a priori judgment.

Kant's answer to Eberhard is that judgments may therefore have attributes as predicates without this fact determining whether the judgment is analytic or synthetic, a priori or a posteriori. But:

> a.   If the predicate signifies an attribute or property of the logical essence, the judgment is analytic and is known a priori.
> b.   If the predicate signifies a property or accident learned by experience of an object, the judgment is synthetic, but is known a posteriori.[75]
> c.   If the predicate signifies an attribute or property of the phenomenal essence as the condition of intuitability, the judgment is synthetic (because the predicate does not follow from the logical essence) and known a priori (because it can be known to apply without appeal to actual experience).[76]

NOTES

1. Lovejoy, "Kant's Antithesis of Dogmatism and Criticism," *Mind*, 1906; reprinted in M. S. Gram, ed., *Kant: Disputed Questions* (Chicago, 1967), pp. 105-30. 1 have examined Lovejoy's paper in considerable detail in "Lovejoy as a Critic of Kant" [cited in Note 74].

2. *Critique of Pure Reason*, B 19; not in A.

3. *Prolegomena*, §3.

4. *Essay*, IV, 8, §§8 and 4. In §3 explicit tautologies are counted among trifling propositions; Kant ("Fortschritte der Metaphysik," Ak. XX, 322) denies that they are analytical: they do not analyze and explicate. He thus distinguishes between judgments based on identity and identical judgments. Only the former are analytical.

5. *Critique of Pure Reason*, A 764-65 = B 792-93.

6. This correspondence has been established, to my satisfaction, by Donald W. Gotterbarn, "Kant, Hume, and Analyticity," *Kant-Studien* 65 (1974), 274-83.

7. Gotterbarn, "Kant, Hume, and Analyticity"; W. A. Suchting, "Hume and Necessary Truth," *Dialogue* (1966-67), 47-60; R. F. Atkinson, "Hume on Mathematics," *Philosophical Quarterly* 10 (1960), 127-37.

8. *Treatise*, ed. Selby-Bigge, p. 95.

9. *Critique of Practical Reason*, Preface, 3rd paragraph from end.

10. *Prolegomena*, Ak. V, 277 (Beck, p. 25).

11. Leibniz usually writes that the predicate is included in the subject, but sometimes that the concept of the predicate is included in (or involved in) the subject concept *(Philosophical Papers and Letters* [trans. Loemker] p. 363; cf. G. H. R. Parkinson, *Logic and Reality in Leibniz's Metaphysics* [Oxford, 1965], pp. 9, 28). Presumably he did not notice the difference, but it permitted him to believe (or shows that he did believe), in

Kant's words, "that he could obtain knowledge of the inner nature of things by comparing all objects merely with the understanding and with the separated, formal concepts of its thought" (*Critique of Pure Reason*, A 270 = B 326). This was, for Kant, "the fundamental mistake of Leibniz" from which the monadology followed (H. J. Paton, "Kant on the Errors of Leibniz," in *Kant Studies Today* [ed. Beck; Lasalle, 1968, pp. 72-87] at p. 75). See also W. E. Abraham, "Complete Concepts and Leibniz's Distinction Between Necessary and Contingent Truths," *Studia Leibnitiana* 1 (1969), 263-79.

12. But Leibniz nevertheless argued that contingent propositions can be known a priori. See discussions of this in Parkinson *Logic and Reality*, p. 66, and Beck, *Early German Philosophy* (Cambridge, 1969), pp. 210-11.

13. *Philosophical Papers and Letters*, p. 286.

14. B. Russell, *Critical Examination of the Philosophy of Leibniz*, p. 20.

15. *New Essays Concerning Human Understanding*, IV, 1, §7.

16. Ibid., IV, 2, §1 (trans. Langley, pp. 404-05). See Margaret Wilson, "On Leibniz's Explication of 'Necessary Truth,'" *Studia Leibnitiana Supplementa* 3 (1969), 50-63.

17. For Leibniz's criticisms of the Hobbesian theory which permitted nominal definitions to suffice, see *Philosophical Papers and Letters*, pp. 199, 355, 371. Against Locke on trifling propositions, see *New Essays*, II, 6, §27; III, 6 §§24 and 32; IV, 5, §§3-8, and Douglas Odegard, "Locke, Leibniz, and Identical Propositions," *Studia Leibnitiana* 1 (1969), 241-53.

18. Russell, *Critical Examination*, p. 18.

19. *Logical Papers*, trans. Parkinson (Oxford, 1966), pp. 64-65.

20. *Prolegomena*, §2.

21. See Gottfried Martin, *Kant: Ontologie und Wissenschaftstheorie* (4th ed., Berlin, 1969), p. 293; Winfried Lenders, *Die analytische Begriffs- und Urteilslehre von Leibniz u. Wolff* (Hildesheim: Olms, 1971), p. 158. On this point alone I disagree with Gram in his excellent introduction to the Lovejoy paper in *Kant: Disputed Questions*, p. 95.

22. *Vernünftige Gedanken von den Kräften des menschlichen Verstandes*, chap. 3, §§1, 2. It is this view which Kant criticizes in *Critique of Pure Reason*, B §19.

23. *Logica*, §§262-64; *Psychologia Empirica*, §369.

24. See the quotation from Lovejoy in Gram, ed., *Kant: Disputed Questions*, 116 n. and the immediately following passages in *Vernünftige Gedanken*, chap. 3, §§10 and 13; also, ibid., chap. 4, §21.

25. *Ontologia*, §48.

26. *Vernünftige Gedanken*, chap. 3, §10.

27. *Critique of Pure Reason*, A 274 = B 330.

28. Lovejoy, "Kant's Antithesis," p. 115.

29. Lambert to Kant, February 3, 1766 (Ak. X, 64; Zweig, *Correspondence*, p. 51).

30. *Vernünftige Gedanken*, chap. 1, §33.

31. *Logica*, §64.

32. *Ontologia*, §170.

33. Ibid., §§89 and 91.

34. Ibid., §92.

35. Lambert certainly did not see this criterion of possibility functioning in Wolff's own mathematics; see Beck, *Early German Philosophy*, p. 404.

36. *Vernünftige Gedanken*, chap. 3, §13; *Logica*, §270.

37. *Logica*, §223.

38. Ibid., §273.

39. Ibid., §223.

40. Lovejoy, "Kant's Antithesis," p. 117.

41. *Logica*, §§220-21.

42. *Vernünftige Gedanken*, chap. 5, §6. Oddly enough, Kant regards the proposition "A triangle possesses three sides and three angles" as analytic (A 716 = B 744). See Gottfried Martin, *Kant: Ontologie*, pp. 276-77.

43. *Vernünftige Gedanken*, chap 4, §21, end.

44. *Ontologia*, §143; cf. §546, note.

45. *Vernünftige Gedanken*, chap. 5, §§6, 7.

46. *Critique of Pure Reason*, B 2.

47. *Vernünftige Gedanken*, chap. 5, §8. Other examples are: "Bodies have weight," and "Air is elastic"—examples Kant himself uses.

48. *Preliminary Discourse on Philosophy in General* (trans. R. J. Blackwell, [Indianapolis, 1963]), §6.

49. Crusius developed an idea which was present in the works of Clauberg, von Tschirnhaus, and Friedrich Adolf Hoffmann (see Beck, *Early German Philosophy*, pp. 185, 191-92, 302-03); later the same way of distinguishing two types of relations was followed by Johann Heinrich Lambert and Johann Heinrich Tetens (ibid., pp. 406-07, 421, 425), but Kant had by then already learned the lesson from Crusius.

50. *Prolegomena*, trans. Beck, p. 8.

51. Letter of August 24, 1793 (Ak. XI, 444-45).

52. *Ontologia*, §70.

53. *Weg zur Gewißheit*, §260.

54. *Entwurf der nothwendigen Vernunftwahrheiten*, §31.

55. Ibid., §15.

56. Letter to Reinhold, May 19, 1789 (Ak. XI, 41; Zweig, *Correspondence*, p. 144); *Reflexionen* 4275 and 4446 (Ak. XVII, 492-554); see also *Vorlesungen über Logik* (Ak. IX, 21).

57. *Versuch den Begriff der negativen Größen in die Weltweisheit einzuführen*, 1763 (Ak. II, 203).

58. Dieter Henrich, "Kants Denken 1762-63: Über den Ursprung der Unterscheidung analytischer und synthetischer Urteile," in *Studien zu Kants philosophischer Entwicklung*, ed. Heimsoeth, Henrich, and Tonelli (Hildesheim, 1967), pp. 9-38; Gottfried Martin, *Kant: Ontologie*, Part 111; Beck, *Early German Philosophy*, pp. 441-46, 451-55.

59. Since this paper was written, Professor Henry E. Allison has published his translation of *Über eine Entdeckung* with supplementary material and a historical and critical commentary: *The Kant-Eberhard Controversy* (Johns Hopkins University Press, 1973).

60. See Beck, *Studies in the Philosophy of Kant*, pp. 81-84 [above, pp. 5-8], 118-20, for comparison of Eberhard's strictures on Kant with those of C. I. Lewis. In [these essays] I deal largely with another problem raised by Maaß, Eberhard, and Lewis, that of the variability and arbitrariness of the distinction between analytic and synthetic, which here I must pass over in silence.

61. Letter to Reinhold, May 12, 1789 (Ak. XI, 38; Zweig, *Correspondence*, p. 141); Allison, *The Kant-Eberhard Controversy*, p. 164.

62. *Analysis of Knowledge and Valuation*, p. 89. S. G. E. Maaß, "Über den höchsten Grundsatz der synthetischen Urtheile," writing in Eberhard's *Philosophisches Magazin* (2

[1790], 186-231 at 197) and Eberhard's ally in the battle, distinguishes between immediate and mediate analytic judgments, corresponding exactly to Lewis's distinction. On
Maaß, see Allison, *The Kant-Eberhard Controversy*, pp. 42-45.

63. *Prolegomena*, §2, a.

64. *Über eine Entdeckung*, Ak. VIII, 230, 242 (Allison, *The Kant-Eberhard Controversy*, pp. 142, 152); Eberhard, "Über die Unterscheidung der Urtheile in Analytische und
Synthetische," *Philosophisches Magazin* 1 (1780), 307-22, at 321.

65. *Critique of Pure Reason*, A 154 = B 193.

66. Eberhard, "Über die analytischen and synthetischen Urtheile zur Beantwortung
des zweyten Abschnittes von H. Prof. Kants Streitschrift," *Philosophisches Magazin* 3
(1791), 280-303 at 282, complains of this, saying that the presence or absence of intuition
has nothing to do with the division of judgments. In "Weitere Ausführung der Unter-
suchung über die Unterscheidung der Urtheile in Analytische and Synthetische," ibid., 2
(1790), 285-315 at 299, Eberhard says that since he is convinced "daß die allgemeinen
Principien der menschlichen Erkenntnis transcendentale Gültigkeit haben: so halte ich
mich berechtigt, so lange mein Beweis von dieser transcendentalen Gültigkeit [sc., of the
principle of sufficient reason derived from the law of contradiction] noch nicht widerlegt
ist, einen jeden logischen Grund auch für einen Realgrund zu halten." It is the thesis of
Lenders's monograph *(Die analytische Begriffs- und Urteilslehre)* that also in Wolff the
ground of distinction among the kinds of judgment is ontological, not epistemological or
logical.

67. *Critique of Pure Reason*, B 40, A 71 = B 96; *Vorlesungen über Logik*, §8; cf.
Vaihinger, *Commentar zu Kants Kritik der reinen Vernunft* I (1881), 258.

68. Kant has often been criticized for holding two criteria of analyticity, the phenomenological or introspective ("actually thought" in the concept of the subject) and the
logical (testable by the law that the contradiction of an analytical judgment is self-contradictory). Here we have a clear indication that when these criteria give conflicting
answers, Kant accepts the latter as prevailing. On the other hand, it is equally clear from
their dispute that, when they conflict, Eberhard must use the former in justifying his
considering a judgment *per attributum* to be synthetic.

69. *Über eine Entdeckung*, Ak. VIII, 230 (Allison, *The Kant-Eberhard Controversy*,
p. 143). The distinction is (naturally) denied by Eberhard in his reply, "Über die analytischen and synthetischen Urtheile, zur Beantwortung des zweyten Abschnittes von H.
Prof. Kants Streitschrift," *Philosophisches Magazin* 3 (1791), 280-303, in particular p.
302.

70. *Critique of Pure Reason*, A 598 = B 626. "Praedicatum logicum kan [sic!] analytisch sein; determinatio est praedicatum syntheticum." Reflexion 5701 (Ak. XVIII,
330).

71. *Über eine Entdeckung*, Ak. VIII, 242 (Allison, *The Kant-Eberhard Controversy*,
p. 152); letter to Reinhold, May 12, 1789 (Zweig, *Correspondence*, p. 140; Allison, *The
Kant-Eberhard Controversy*, pp. 163-64).

72. *Critique of Pure Reason*, A 292 = B 348.

73. Ibid., A 218 = B 265.

74. Kant may perhaps have confused Eberhard by calling real essence "die innere
Möglichkeit des Begriffes" or "interna possibilitas" and distinguishing it from the "logisches Wesen" (*Über eine Entdeckung*, Ak. VIII, 229). By "innere Möglichkeit des Begriffes" he actually means "innere Möglichkeit *des Objektes* des Begriffes." This is made
clear in the manuscripts Kant prepared to help Schulz in Schulz's reply to Eberhard (Ak.

XX, 376, first full paragraph); similar usage in *Vorlesungen über Logik* (Ak. IX, 61); *Vorlesungen über Metaphysik* (ed. Pölitz, 1821), p. 38; *Critique of Pure Reason*, A 676 = B 703; A 816 = B 844. *Einzig möglicher Beweisgrund* (Ak. II, 77-78, 162) distinguishes "innere Möglichkeit" from "das Logische in der Möglichkeit" and identifies the former with the "Wesen der Dinge." I have examined all these passages in "Lovejoy as a Critic of Kant," [*Journal of the History of Ideas* 33 (1972), pp. 471-84, in particular pp. 482-83; rpt. in Beck, *Essays on Kant and Hume* (New Haven: Yale, 1978), pp. 61-79, in particular pp. 76-77].

75. *Critique of Pure Reason*, A 728=B 756.

76. [This essay originally appeared in W. H. Werkmeister, ed., *Reflections on Kant's Philosophy* (Gainesville: University Presses of Florida, 1975), pp. 7-27, and is reprinted with the permission of the University Press of Florida.]

On the Putative Apriority of Judgments of Taste

Kant says that "we desire that judgments of experience shall always hold good for us and in the same way for everyone else,"[1] and we consider a judgment of experience as "valid and hence necessary."[2] "Necessary," however, does not mean a priori; it means merely universally valid, having a legitimate claim upon the credence of every competent observer: "The objective validity of the judgment of experience means nothing other than its necessary universal validity [*Allgemeingültigkeit*]."[3] "The sun warms the stone" is not an a priori but an empirical judgment; if it is true that the sun does warm the stone, however, then it is necessary for everyone who judges to judge that the sun does warm the stone. What makes this necessary is an a priori judgment, namely the Second Analogy of Experience, applied to observational evidence.

A like argument in the *Critique of Judgment*, however, leads Kant to say of judgments of taste that they are not merely necessary but a priori, "or are held to be such."[4] This is surely wrong, and resembles a like confusion in the first *Critique* (A 104) between the two senses of "necessary," only one of which is equivalent to "a priori." "This arabesque is beautiful" is no more a priori than "The sun warms the stone." What is a priori in the latter is the presupposed Analogy of Experience, in the former "the a priori principles of pure *Urteilskraft* in aesthetic *Urteilen*."[5] What seems to have led Kant astray here is that there is an a priori relation between the judgment of beauty and the claim to universal (that is to say, necessary) validity. "It is an empirical judgment that I perceive and estimate an object with pleasure. It is, however, an apriori judgment that I find it beautiful, *that is* that I may attribute that delight to everyone as necessary."[6] The "that is" (*d.i.*) should be "therefore" (*daher*), and while the whole sentence put into hypothetical form may be a priori, the protasis is not.[7]

It would be odd, in Kant's usage certainly, to admit that an a priori judgment could be wrong. Yet unless there is some standard for assessing a judgment, that is to say, unless the judgment first is "necessary" in contrast to "arbitrary," the judgment cannot be said to be right *or* wrong. The first standard is that of *Allgemeingültigkeit* (universal validity). It is frequently said (though not by Kant)[8] that Theaetetan judgments are incorrigible because they do not make a claim that can be assessed, but they nevertheless may be false (because I can lie or make a verbal error). But an objective judgment of experience makes a claim, whether it be true or false; in fact, it makes the *same* claim whether it be true or false. The conditions of cognitive validity are independent of the truth or falsity of what is claimed.[9] Thus "The sun warms the stone" is objectively valid (makes a necessary claim upon our credence and ratification) even though it is not a priori and may, in fact, not be true.

Once we see that Kant's judgments of taste are not comparable to a priori cognitive judgments but to objective empirical cognitive judgments (= objectively valid judgments of experience), we can understand the way in which judgments of taste can be *valid but erroneous* while they could hardly be *a priori but erroneous.*

Critical disputes presuppose the distinction between judgments of agreeableness (like judgments of sensation) and judgments of taste (like judgments of experience), and the a priori ascription of validity to the latter. Disputes about them are only about whether "the correct application of the faculty of taste" has been made.[10] One who makes a judgment of taste is a "suitor for agreement from everyone else" and is "able to count on this agreement" provided the case being judged does fall under the conditions of aesthetic approval.[11] The judgment, "The arabesque is beautiful," is not and does not imply the empirical judgment, "The arabesque is liked by everyone." It does not *postulate* the agreement but *imputes* it *(sinnt nur jedermann diese Einstimmung ein).*[12] Thus "The arabesque is beautiful" is not refuted by "Mr. X does not like it." Nonetheless I may judge "That nude is beautiful," not meaning merely that I (and others) *like* it, and yet make an aesthetic error. How?

The grounds of erroneous judgments of taste are very much like those of erroneous cognitive and moral judgments, all of which are necessary (in the sense defined) and none of which (as singular judgments of specific cases) is a priori.

a. *Cognitive error* arises "from the unobserved influence of sensibility on the understanding, whereby it happens that the subjective grounds of judgment enter into union with the objective grounds and make these latter deviate from their true functions."[13]

b. *Moral error* is possible for "we cannot by any means conclude with certainty that a secret impulse of self-love falsely appearing as the idea of duty was not actually the true determining ground of the Will."[14]

c. *Error in taste* arises from sinning against the conditions of aesthetic validity,[15] especially the condition of the disinterestedness of the pleasure (like the disinterestedness of motive in morality). A "taint" of empirical delight is always present "where charm or emotion have a share in the judgment by which something is to be described as beautiful."[16, 17]

NOTES

1. *Prolegomena*, §18.
2. Ibid., §19.
3. Ibid., §18 (Ak. IV, 298).
4. *Critique of Judgment*, §36 (Ak. V, 289; Meredith, p. 145).
5. Ibid., §36 (Ak. V, 288; Meredith, p. 144).
6. *Critique of Judgment*, §37 (Ak. V, 289; Meredith, p. 146).
7. If C. I. Lewis's claim (*Analysis of Knowledge and Valuation*, pp. 161-62) is sound that the Second Analogy is analytical of the "concept of objective event," it might be argued that the definition of the beautiful drawn from the Second Moment of Quantity, viz., "The *beautiful* is that which apart from a concept, pleases universally" (*Critique of*

Judgment, §19), makes even the claim by Kant in §36 that the principles of aesthetic judgment are *synthetic* false.

8. Though he comes near doing so: the senses do not deceive, for the senses do not judge (*Critique of Pure Reason*, A 293-94 = B 350).

9. Gerold Prauss, *Erscheinung bei Kant* (Berlin, 1971), p. 86.

10. *Critique of Judgment* §8 (Ak. V, 214; Meredith, p. 54).

11. Ibid., §22 (Ak. V, 239; Meredith, p. 85).

12. Ibid., §8 (Ak. V, 216; Meredith, p. 55).

13. *Critique of Pure Reason*, A 295 = B 350-51.

14. *Foundations of the Metaphysics of Morals*, II, second paragraph.

15. *Critique of Judgment*, §8, end.

16. Ibid., §14 (Ak. V, 224; Meredith, p. 65).

17. [This essay originally appeared in *bewußt sein, Gerhard Funke zu eigen* (Bonn: Bouvier, 1975), and is reprinted with permission.]

A Non Sequitur of Numbing Grossness?

In 1902 Lovejoy pointed out what he considered to be "one of the most spectacular examples of the *non-sequitur* which are to be found in the history of philosophy."[1] Nobody took any notice. In 1966, commenting on the very same passage in the *Critique of Pure Reason,* Strawson called it "a *non sequitur* of numbing grossness."[2] This caused a flurry of responses by *echt-Kantianer,* none of which seems to me to be satisfactory. The sudden thrust of the Lovejoy-Strawson argument has not been parried, but only muffled in the cloak of the transcendental philosophy as a whole. Believing that the effective refutation of an argument should not be significantly longer or any less clear than the argument itself, I shall try to deal with it in its own terms, in a paper not disproportionately longer or more piously Kantian.

The *non sequitur* which Lovejoy and Strawson claim to find at A 192-3 = B 237-38 is as follows. From the irreversibility of the sequence of perceptions of states of an object, we infer that the states of the object are themselves in a sequence which is irreversible. That surely would be a *non sequitur.* The question is: is this Kant's inference? I shall try to show that it is not, or at least that perplexing obscurities of his argument allow, if not require, an interpretation which does not contain this *non sequitur.* Then I shall try to show why Strawson thought Kant's argument did.

In reconstructing Kant's argument, I shall make use of one or two points Kant makes clear only by additions made in the Second Edition, perhaps because he saw that the first proof in the First Edition was vulnerable to criticism.

I reconstruct the argument as follows:

1. That the state A in the object precedes the state B in the object (that is to say, that the objective event symbolized as [AB] occurs) is a sufficient condition, given perceptual isomorphism,[3] for the irreversibility of the sequence of the perceptual representations of the states A and B. (The sequence of representations is symbolized as $[A_rB_r]$.)

2. But knowledge of $[A_rB_r]$-irreversibly is not a sufficient condition for knowledge that [AB] occurs, and *a fortiori* not a sufficient condition for knowledge that [AB]-irreversibly occurs. For:

(i) It could be the case that A and B are coexistent but such as to be always perceived in the order $[A_rB_r]$, which is interpreted as $[A_rB_r]$-irreversibly; or

(ii) It could be the case that B precedes A, if perceptual isomorphism fails.

3. In order to know, or to have good reason to believe, that [AB] occurs, given knowledge of $[A_rB_r]$-irreversibly, I must know or have good reason to believe both that:

(i) A and B are opposite states of a substance (B 233), in order to rule out 2 (i); and

(ii) [AB]-irreversibly, in order to rule out 2 (ii).

4. Knowledge of, or a sufficient reason to believe, 3 (i) is sufficient reason to know or justifiably believe that there is an event (a change of states of an object) but not sufficient reason to know or believe that the event is [AB] and not [BA] (B 233).

5. But I know, or have sufficient reason to believe, that [AB] occurs.

6. Therefore I know, or have sufficient reason to believe, that [AB]-irreversibly occurs (3, [ii]).

7. [AB] -irreversibly is the schema of causation.

8. Therefore to know, or to have sufficient reason to believe, that [AB] occurs, I must know, or have sufficient reason to believe, that A is, or contains, a causal condition of B.

I shall now briefly comment upon several of these steps.

ad 1. Kant says (A 193 = B 238) we must derive (*ableiten*) [A_rB_r] (and perhaps even [A_rB_r]-irreversibly) from [AB]. But surely he means merely that [A_rB_r] and [A_rB_r]-irreversibly are dependent upon [AB]; any sequence of representations is *given*, not *derived* in any sense of "concluded."

ad 2. The denial of this is the *non sequitur* ascribed to Kant. But 2 is explicitly stated at B 234: "The *objective relation* of appearances [that is, of A and B] that follow upon one another is not to be determined through mere perception [that is, from the sequential relation of A_r and B_r]." Hence Kant does not claim that [A_rB_r]-irreversibly entails [AB].

ad 2 (i). The world might be so constituted that all its parts are coexistent but (for some queer reason) they can be perceived only in an irreversible sequence of representations. To use Kant's example of the house: maybe there is a house so situated that, as I approach it by the only road leading to it, I always see the roof before seeing the windows, and the east side before the west side. Let us suppose this is my reason for (incorrectly) asserting [A_rB_r]-irreversibly. But I would be wrong, *ex hypothesi*, in interpreting the putative [A_rB_r]-irreversibly as evidence for [AB].

ad 2 (ii). Perceptual isomorphism fails when, for example, I cannot but see an eclipse of the moon before I see the explosion of a nova, even though the nova exploded thousands of years before the eclipse occurred.[4] But unless I know that [AB] and not [BA] occurs, I cannot discover the absence of perceptual isomorphism. It is knowledge of a law of nature, for example, a law concerning the necessary sequence of positions of states of the wave-front of a light-ray, which requires me to say that [BA] occurred *in spite of* [A_rB_r]-irreversibly. In other words, at least causal laws of nature must be posited in order to know how to interpret [A_rB_r]-irreversibly. In order to know the objective order of the two events, "the relation between the two states must be so thought that it is thereby determined as necessary which of them must be placed before, and which after, and that they cannot be placed in the reverse relation" (B 234).

ad 5. Kant says, "I see a ship move down stream." Paton correctly pointed out that this is an independent premise of Kant's argument.[5] [AB] is not an intermediate step in an invalid inference from [A$_r$B$_r$]-irreversibly to [AB]-irreversibly; *that* line of argument has been ruled out by 2. Still, one may ask whether Kant had a right to this premise; perhaps all he could claim to know was [A$_r$B$_r$]. If I am correct in seeing the argument here as a response to Hume,[6] however, Kant has a right to any premise which Hume has made use of in his argument against the causal principle. Hume assumed that he knew [AB] because he had, from repetition of cases like [AB], explained how the illusion arises that [AB]-necessarily. Kant's entire argument against Hume at this point and at A 196 = B 241 takes the following form: Hume knows [AB] but has skeptical doubts about [AB]-necessarily. But unless one knows, or has reason to believe, [AB]-irreversibly, then [A$_r$B$_r$], and even [A$_r$B$_r$]-irreversibly, is not good evidence for [AB]. *If* one knows [AB], therefore, he has good reason for asserting what Hume denied, namely [AB]-irreversibly.

ad 7. You will notice that in the previous note, when dealing with Hume I wrote [...]-necessarily, and when dealing with Kant I wrote [...]-irreversibly. The reason for this is that while the concept of causal connection is the concept of [AB]-necessarily, the schema of the concept is [AB]-irreversibly. While Kant's statement of the schema of causation at A 144 = B 183 does not absolutely rule out the interpretation of the schema as being [A$_r$B$_r$]-irreversibly, it is clear that in the Second Analogy he means [AB]-irreversibly, for he says, "The sequence in time is thus the sole empirical criterion of an effect in its relation to the causality of the cause which precedes it."

There is nothing in this argument which requires that our knowledge-claim that [AB]-irreversibly be true. It is sufficient against Hume that it must be assumed in justification of Hume's knowledge claim that [AB] occurs.

I shall now comment upon why I think Strawson has misinterpreted Kant's argument, especially why I think he has misread part of A 193 / B 238 (in Kemp Smith, p. 222, lines 2-12).

Van Cleve points out that Strawson has written his criticism from a "realistic" view.[7] According to that view, A and B and the substance of which they are states are ontologically real, independent of any construction; they are not mere phenomena "under a law given them by the understanding." If it is a fact about the world that [AB] occurs, and if in order to know it we do not have to "constitute" it or ground our knowledge of it except by adducing the evidence [A$_r$B$_r$]-irreversibly, then there is no way to go from [A$_r$B$_r$]-irreversibly to [AB]-irreversibly. Given this conception of the object and our knowledge of it, Van Cleve is correct in ratifying Strawson's accusation, for the Kantian "proof" stops at [AB] and does not reach [AB]-irreversibly.

But we must notice that Kant was aware of that, and could riposte on Strawson that, given *that* conception of object, he and Strawson could not reach even [AB] from [A$_r$B$_r$]-irreversibly. For, he says "If appearances [sc. objects and their states] were things in themselves...we could never determine from the succession of representations how their manifold may be connected *in the object*" (A 190 / B 235, italics added). Now it is reasonable to suppose that Kant would not then immediately employ a concept of object which he had just seen would render his own argument invalid.

And we have to look only to the end of the paragraph from which I have just quoted, which immediately precedes the passages which are in dispute, to find Kant's own definition of object: it is "*that* in the appearance which contains the condition of this necessary rule of apprehension."[8] The rule for constituting (constructing) an object specifies necessary temporal relations. The rule is a priori, even though in any particular case we may not know, and certainly do not know a priori, what the *specific* temporal relation is between *specific* states.

Accordingly, Kant distinguishes two kinds of objects, the possibility of knowledge of which is constituted by the application of one or the other of two rules. They are: permanent stable objects, like the house, and objects undergoing a change, like the ship. Each fits the broad definition of "object" quoted above. The second object is posited on the evidence of [A_rB_r]-irreversibly under the (meta-)rule stated in the Second Analogy: "Everything that happens, that is, begins to be, presupposes something upon which it follows according to a rule."

Thus to know [AB] I must employ not merely the evidence [A_rB_r]-irreversibly but also the rule that whichever state comes first does so according to a rule by which a changing object is posited. I do not know that some specific A precedes necessarily some specific B; I might even be wrong in thinking A precedes B at all. But if I know [AB] on the evidence [A_rB_r]-irreversibly, then I must follow the rule that the earlier state is, or contains, the condition of the later. This meta-rule for the specific empirically founded rule "[AB]-irreversibly" is the condition under which alone I can distinguish between stable objects and changing objects or objective events, since the evidence [A_rB_r]-irreversibly does not suffice.

"[AB]-irreversibly" is the rule that Kant obscurely refers to, or meant to refer to, at A 193 = B 238 (Kemp Smith, p. 222, line 11), not "[A_rB_r]-irreversibly", for the latter is not a rule but only evidence to be used according to a rule. To infer the former from the latter would indeed be a *non sequitur* of numbing grossness.[9]

NOTES

1. A. O. Lovejoy, "On Kant's Reply to Hume," *Archiv für Geschichte der Philosophie* (1906), reprinted in M. S. Gram, ed., *Kant: Disputed Questions* (Chicago, 1967), p. 303.

2. P. F. Strawson, *The Bounds of Sense* (London, 1966), p. 137.

3. The term is borrowed from James Van Cleve, "Four Recent Interpretations of Kant's Second Analogy," *Kant-Studien* 64 (1973), pp. 71-87, at p. 81. But I use the term to refer only to the condition that there be no relevant difference in the modes of causal

dependence of A$_r$ on A and of B$_r$ on B. See [Beck, *Essays on Kant and Hume* (New Haven: Yale, 1978), p. 161.]

4. Kant talks about the sequence of states in a substance and not the sequence of events. His model of causation is Leibnizian, not Humean. (If one remembers this there is no danger in using examples like the eclipse and the nova, which more readily fit into a Humean than into a Leibnizian pattern. Kant will extend his model in the Third Analogy; but nothing relevant to the present controversy depends upon the choice of a Leibnizian or Humean model and example.)

5. H. J. Paton, *Kant's Metaphysic of Experience* (London, 1936), II, 240.

6. As I argue in "Once More Unto the Breach: Kant's Answer to Hume, Again" [above, pp. 69-72].

7. Van Cleve, "Four Recent Interpretations," p. 84.

8. Similar definitions at A 104, A 106, and B 137.

9. [This essay originally appeared in *Kant-Studien* 67 (1976), pp. 385-89, and is reprinted with permission.]

.

www.ingramcontent.com/pod-product-compliance
Lightning Source LLC
Chambersburg PA
CBHW020702030726
47498CB00002B/600